PRIMARY WRITING

PRIMARY WRITING

Dominic Wyse

OPEN UNIVERSITY PRESS
Buckingham · Philadelphia

Open University Press
Celtic Court
22 Ballmoor
Buckingham
MK18 1XW

e-mail: enquiries@openup.co.uk
world wide web: http://www.openup.co.uk

and
325 Chestnut Street
Philadelphia, PA 19106, USA

First Published 1998

A catalogue record of this book is available from the British Library

ISBN 0 335 19813 9 (pb)   0335 19814 7 (hb)

Library of Congress Cataloging-in-Publication Data
Wyse, Dominic, 1964–
      Primary writing / Dominic Wyse.
         p.   cm.
      Includes bibliographical references (p.) and index.
      ISBN 0–335–19814–7 (hbk)   ISBN 0–335–19813–9 (pbk)
      1. English language—Composition and exercises—Study and teaching
   (Elementary)—Great Britain.   I. Title.
   LB1576.W97   1998
   372.62'3'044—dc21   97–40295
                                                                          CIP

Typeset by Type Study, Scarborough
Printed in Great Britain by St Edmundsbury Press, Bury St Edmunds, Suffolk

Contents

Acknowledgements

Grateful thanks to Barrie, Vera, Angela, Jim, Brenda, Jane, Andy, Ruth, John and Judith for commenting on drafts of various chapters and involvement in the research. Last but not least to Jackie for her many hours of support and encouragement.

The article from the Halifax *Evening Courier* by Cathy O'Connor is reproduced with permission (page *43*).

The composition/transcription table on page 36 is reproduced from *Writing and the Writer* by Frank Smith, by permission of Heinemann Educational Publishers.

Introduction

The 'process approach' to the teaching of primary writing is a term that has been regularly used in the UK. Although there have been some good descriptions and examples of classroom practice, there has been little information on the process approach in the context of the whole school. The information that is available offers little advice or reflection on the development of the approach over a number of years, on how schools can take a unified approach, or on what the future direction for the process approach might be.

At this point you might expect me to offer a succinct definition of the process approach. I will attempt to sum up some of the significant features but, to a certain extent, all the chapters of the book contribute to a composite picture of the approach. The process approach is typified by several key features within the classroom and the whole school:

- In the classroom the teacher establishes a developing community of young writers; most of those writers are offered high levels of control over the process of writing; children's earliest attempts at mark-making are seen as writing; the writing develops within a publishing cycle that mirrors aspects of the publication processes in the world outside the classroom.
- It is implemented as a commonly understood approach throughout the school; children's learning from nursery to Year 6 is seen as a continuum of development; the underlying philosophies have an impact on reading, writing and other areas of the curriculum.

The process approach is not simply a method that one can select as part of what Browne (1996: 25) calls a 'pick-and-mix' approach.

The relationship between theory and practice continues to be debated in primary education. Throughout the book I have tried to steer a course which gives the appropriate balance between them. The book centres mainly on practice, and this is reflected in the balance of the chapters and the descriptions which illustrate the points I put forward. However, I feel strongly that good practice should be underpinned by sound theoretical perspectives, so most of the chapters have a clearly identified 'theory and research' section that makes reference to a range of research and publication related to the issues covered in those chapters. In addition, the final chapter looks in more depth at some of the research, publication and theories related to the process approach, and particularly the work of Donald Graves. The decision to make a clear separation rather than integrate the theory in an ongoing way is intended to allow readers to access those sections that are most relevant to them at the time of reading.

The work of the New Zealand researcher and teacher Donald Graves has had a strong influence on my own experience and the writing of the book; this influence began some ten years ago. During my first year of teaching I taught in a deprived area of inner London. Every Sunday night I planned the week's activities, paying particular attention to the writing tasks because writing had been an interest at college. Over the first six months I began to realize that in spite of the wide range of writing tasks I planned for the children, they were clearly not particularly motivated. I could see in some of the faces the thought, 'Oh no, not writing again.' At this time I attended one of the many excellent courses that were run on a weekly basis for probationary teachers working for the Inner London Education Authority (ILEA). One of the advisory teachers recommended the work of Donald Graves, and I was immediately struck by the power of his ideas. Having looked at Graves's work I decided to initiate a regular writing workshop; I did not need to read the children's faces because they would say things like, 'When are we doing writing workshop again?' or, 'Is it writing workshop today?' Throughout the book I draw heavily on my professional experience. I have done this because the experience allows me to comment in depth on the process approach by reflecting upon eight years of primary teaching experience in three authorities, and my role as language coordinator in two markedly different schools. I did not set out to present the experiences of many different schools, although I do draw on the experiences of a wide range of other teachers, some of whom commented on the early drafts of this text.

The impact of reading Donald Graves's work resulted in a primary school teaching career where the process approach was always a feature of my classroom practice both as an infant and as a junior teacher. As a language coordinator I found that colleagues were also interested in the process approach and were keen to include it as part of whole school policy. More recently, as a researcher the process approach has influenced my choice of research and the methods that I used.

The aim of the book is to offer an in-depth account of the process approach in practice and theory, and to suggest some of the potentially wide-ranging implications that adoption of the approach can have. *Primary Writing* is the first book-length treatment of the subject in the UK.

ONE

Writing workshop

The use of writing workshop as a teaching strategy epitomizes some of the most important aspects of the process approach to primary writing. Some people have even argued that writing workshop is synonymous with the process approach. I will suggest throughout the book that the approach is much broader in its scope than writing workshop alone; however, the use of writing workshop is an important feature.

This chapter is divided into two sections. The first half covers some of the important practical decisions that have to be made by the teacher, such as classroom organization, generating ideas, interaction, the publishing cycle, and recording development. The second half of the chapter analyses some children's texts that were produced during writing workshop, and discusses the issues they raised.

Writing workshop is a whole class teaching session where all the children are encouraged to write. The motivation for this comes about mainly through the freedom of choice children are offered over their writing. The workshop is influenced by the natural audiences that are available in the classroom and wider community. A publishing cycle is initiated in the classroom, with the children's completed books becoming part of the class reading area, and these books are subject to all the typical interaction surrounding professionally produced books. The main audience for the children's books is their peers, although the teacher, family and friends, other children in the school, parents, other teachers and other school children are all potential audiences for the writers. Teaching takes place at the beginning of the session in the form of 'mini-lessons', in 'writing conferences' with individual children throughout, and the whole class sharing time at the end of the session.

Classroom organization

Teacher: As you know, this morning is writing workshop.
Various children: Yesss!

	Yes! I've got this idea . . .
	What are you gonna do? [excited whispering]
Teacher:	I'm sure you all missed school when it was closed because of the snow!
Children:	Yeah, yeah . . .
Saiba:	[Aside] I did, I wanted to do writing workshop.

The extract above typifies the kind of enjoyment that children get from successful writing workshop organization. Writing workshop is a good motivator primarily because it puts the children in control of their learning in a genuine way. The decisions over what to write and how to write it are primarily made by the pupils themselves. However, great skill, sensitivity, meticulous organization and flexibility are required by the teacher.

First and foremost the children need the basic equipment. Various sizes of paper need to be carefully stored, clearly labelled and accessible. Large sheets of lined paper are ideal for early drafts, plain A4 paper, A5 paper and card for bookmaking; a labelled standard drawer unit provides useful storage for paper. For younger children, simple booklets can be made in advance; however, the predetermined number of pages can detract from an important part of the decision-making process. The decision on where the writing and illustrations from a first draft should fit in the final book can be an important learning experience. The children also need access to pens, pencils, felt pens, calligraphy materials, word processors, etc.

Each child should have a writing folder. This folder contains the drafts of the writing that they are currently working on. School exercise books are inappropriate if they are used for other tasks as well (writing workshop texts can become rather disjointed if sandwiched between various other bits of work), but when used as a notebook for early drafts from writing workshop they can be helpful.

The workshop needs to be timetabled so that it happens at the same time each week and for a set amount of time. This is important, as it gives the children the opportunity to be thinking about ideas they would like to try in advance. The composer Stravinsky was once asked how much music writing he did each day. He replied 'I work bank hours, nine till three-thirty. The rest of the time I am thinking about what I shall do next.' Some children are fortunate enough to have typewriters and word processing facilities at home. This gives them the opportunity to work on early drafts at home and bring them to school for writing workshop.

The first few workshops need to concentrate on developing the routines which will sustain the process throughout the year. The most important of these is the idea that children must be prepared to have a go. They must be able to take risks, and they need to view the first draft as an opportunity to get ideas down on paper, with subsequent drafts giving the opportunity to tackle transcription problems such as spelling, punctuation, presentation etc. One of the potential hurdles for many children is spelling. The writing workshop will not function if children are continually stopping for spellings. The invented spelling approach is vital if the positive atmosphere of the workshop is to be achieved. (For more on the implications of invented spelling see Chapter 4.)

Generating ideas

Some teachers find problematic the idea that children can generate their own writing tasks. It is sometimes claimed that this does not provide enough structure and that children are unable to make appropriate choices. These arguments can be countered in two ways. Teachers who have adopted workshop approaches have found that most children can generate interesting, challenging and appropriate ideas for writing, but there will always be a minority of children who require a greater level of support from the teacher; in addition, most children may encounter periods when they are stuck for ideas, where they need a greater level of support than usual. The second point is that the writing workshop is not the only form of organization for writing. There will be many other structured written tasks going on during the week. These will be part of other National Curriculum planning, including skill based writing tasks. However, the workshop is important because it can particularly help the children understand more about the compositional concepts associated with the process of writing. The workshop is set in a context where purpose and audience are determined by the writer. The understanding of these elements serves to broaden the pupil's thinking.

One of the most effective ways to help the child to generate an idea for a piece of writing is a simple list. The pupil who is struggling for an idea is encouraged to note down the first idea which comes into his/her mind. This process is repeated at least five times, with each idea completely different from the one before. For some children the teacher can act as scribe, particularly if the act of writing itself is so difficult for the child that it slows and restricts the ideas. The child is then encouraged to choose their favourite from the ideas on the list. Sometimes this listing process helps the pupil to recognize those ideas that they do *not* want to write about, and they quickly decide to follow up a different line of thought.

The following example of a brainstorm was produced in a writing workshop. Lorraine had decided she wanted to write a story, but could not settle on a good idea. The teacher suggested she write a list. He pushed her to speak quickly and not worry about how ridiculous the idea seemed at first. The other children at her table also contributed possible ideas.

1 Horror story
2 Two bears
3 The stolen cars
4 Pepsi Max maniac
5 The ghost walk

Lorraine decided to use the third and fourth ideas in the list for a book featuring two short stories.

Pupils who have written many books over a long period of time can sometimes feel lost for ideas. It can help to discuss the range of forms and genres that are available to them. The decision to write an information book or a book of poetry or a magazine can help to narrow the field of choice for the pupil, making the task seem much more manageable. Sometimes it is necessary to break down the particular genre and consider the types of text that are associated with it, as a reminder of the range of possibilities that is available. There are a number of other planning models which children can use; but the two most important decisions the young writer needs to make are: 'What is my idea for writing?' and 'Who am I writing it for?'

Interaction

The writing workshop naturally utilizes the various ways of grouping children. Whole class discussion is used at the beginning and end of the workshop. During the workshop the majority of children work individually; however, the flexibility exists for groups of children to collaborate. The various groupings call on the teacher to offer different styles of interaction. Calkins (1986) is also a strong proponent of the writing workshop approach. The basic principles such as student choice, the importance of conferencing, the publishing cycle in the classroom etc she shares with Graves (1983). Where she offers something distinctive is with regard to the use of mini-lessons.

Mini-lessons

The beginning of the workshop is often initiated by a mini-lesson on some aspect of the writing process. These are reasonably formal sessions where the teacher may use a flipchart or wall board to illustrate to the whole class various issues that have arisen. The first of the new year will be used as a way of reminding children of the purposes and routines behind the workshop. Other mini-lessons throughout the year will be structured according to the particular needs of the class. As an illustration of the possibilities, here are some of the more common mini-lessons.

Shared writing
The shared writing strategy is used. The teacher asks the children to contribute sentences for a collaborative text in order to model the process of writing and focus on composition. As the children become more experienced, various other aspects can be covered such as initial letter strategies, phonic knowledge, concept of word and space etc.

Topic choice
Early in the year the teacher asks pupils to brainstorm ideas for writing. This supports the children who may struggle for ideas. As the year progresses, this kind of session serves to remind everyone of the potential wealth of ideas that are being written about at any one time. (Later in the chapter there is an example of the range of topic choices that were being made by one class.)

Finished writing
One of the difficulties can be knowing when a text is finished and what to do next. Children are offered strategies to deal with this. First and foremost they are shown how to become good at redrafting and proofreading their own work; this can be modelled by the teacher using the flipchart. The children's

peers can also be a good source of advice, although they need training to offer appropriate feedback. The final stage involves consulting the teacher, who offers advice on changes where necessary, or recommends publication of the book.

Classroom processes
The writing workshop requires children to equip themselves with all the necessary materials such as bookmaking resources, artwork resources, pencils, pens, paper, dictionaries etc. They need to be made aware of efficient class-room routines such as bookmaking procedures, the use of line guides, types of paper, the clearest pens, effective lettering and so on.

Redrafting strategies
Even experienced children have problems with redrafting for meaning and not just for the technical things such as spelling and punctuation. The idea that writers often redraft many times and make decisions on the most appropriate language to use is one that children develop slowly and with much input from their teacher. (There is a more detailed example of this at the end of this list of mini-lessons.)

What is good writing?
This is an area which tends to spread to reading conferences as well. All the issues surrounding 'quality' texts and 'popular' texts can be usefully analysed as a way of developing higher order thinking skills and to help the children improve the quality of their writing. More specific lessons can teach the use of descriptive language, simile and metaphor, characterization, recurring themes etc. The following two passages from children's novels were used as a starting point for a discussion about 'quality' and 'popular' texts. The teacher had written both examples onto the flipchart. She did not intend to make a judgement about the texts, but wanted the children to be aware of some of the issues and offer their own preferences.

> The Iron Man came to the top of the cliff. How far had he walked? Nobody knows. Where had he come from? Nobody knows. How was he made? Nobody knows.
>
> Taller than a house, the Iron Man stood at the top of the cliff, on the very brink, in the darkness.
>
> The wind sang through his iron fingers. His great iron head shaped like a dustbin but as big as a bedroom, slowly turned to the right, slowly turned to the left. His iron ears turned this way, that way. He was hearing the sea.
>
> (*The Iron Man* by Ted Hughes)

> Later, when Belinda thought about that horrible night, she could think of a hundred 'if onlys' that might have made things turn out differently. If only we hadn't gone to that party . . . She hated parties anyway, and Hildy had been grounded – why in the world had she ever told Hildy she'd go along in the first place? She hadn't even known the people who'd been giving the stupid party – some college buddies of Frank's older brother –

and once she and Hildy and Frank had gotten there, she'd known right away that there was too much drinking going on.

(*April Fools* by Richie Tankersley Cusick)

The teacher asked the children to read both passages as she read them aloud. She explained that she wanted them to think about the different ways they were written. Here are some of the children's comments:

'The Iron Man sounds like poetry because bits are repeated.'
'There's better description in the Iron Man. The parts of the body are described really well.'
'I liked *April Fools* best because it is happening now and the other book is about robots.'
'The next paragraph in *April Fools* has a car crash and that was exciting. It wasn't fair to only compare one paragraph.'

Transcription

The teacher will observe children at work and become aware of the skills which the children need. For younger children, knowing where to put capital letters and full stops, and the concept of sentence, is a common issue. This can be illustrated on the flipchart by encouraging the class to correct a text where the capitals and full stops have been omitted. For older children, how to use speech marks is a regular focus, particularly knowing when to start new lines etc.

To illustrate one of the mini-lessons in more depth I show how one teacher interpreted 'redrafting strategies'. The teacher had set up an activity for the children which involved the 'Bauplay' construction equipment. This has various large brick shapes, cogs, nuts and bolts, wheels etc. When the children had made a model he photographed their work as a record. Subsequently he asked the children to write a description of how they made the model and what it was for. This was to accompany the photograph for a display. One of these descriptions formed the basis for his mini-lesson prior to the writing workshop the following day. The first draft of Christopher's writing was transferred to the flipchart. The children were asked to offer suggestions as to how they would redraft the writing. They were asked to think about sentences that could be changed, as well as single words. The following text shows the original in ordinary type and the children's suggested changes and insertions in italics.

The Machine Robot   *and*   *any shops that*
It does washing and ironing ∧ you can buy new parts from <u>anywhere you can</u>
sell   *Richard and I built*   *using*
<u>buy</u> 'Bauplay'. This is how we made it. <u>Me and Richard made</u> it by <u>building</u>
           bolting
different parts and then <u>putting</u> them together. It was originally meant to
      We changed it because we wanted a wheel to fall off the machine
      to make an alarm sound. We found this was too difficult.
be an alarm system. ∧ The things we made it with were: wheels, cogs, tubes, screws, connectors, handles and long/short joins.

Writing conference

Arguably the most important part of the writing workshop is the writing conference. This is a period of one-to-one teacher/pupil interaction where the two discuss the writing in progress. It is a time when skill and perceptiveness are required on the part of the teacher. If the interaction is to be effective, the teacher needs to be able to anticipate the many possible types of writing that pupils will be involved in at any one time. Not only will the teacher need to make recommendations on the compositional aspects of the piece, but he/she will also need to consider how to offer feedback on the wide range of transcription skills which the pupil may need help with. All pupils work at their natural developmental level, and this is reflected in the skills they use as well as in the compositional choices they make.

The teacher's response to the piece of writing is the crucial element of the conference. Generally this will be dependent on the individual pupil's needs, their age, and the nature of the relationship that has been developed between teacher and pupil. As a rule of thumb I would offer the following guidelines for interaction:

1 Respond to the compositional elements of the piece of writing by praising something you like and/or by asking a question about something that is of genuine interest to you.
2 Help to improve one compositional element.
3 Help to improve one transcriptional element.

Teaching and learning is never that simple, of course. For some children whom the teacher knows well and who are confident, the teacher may choose to focus immediately on a particular skill that he/she has been developing with that child over a period of time. For others, discussion of skills needs to be postponed until the teacher has developed the child's confidence by offering positive feedback and by focusing on the compositional aspects. Some children may benefit from the teacher editing, proofreading and correcting their work ready for final draft and publication, with minimal comment. This may also be the case if the teacher feels the writing is effective and is at the highest standard for the particular pupil at that time.

The interaction of writing conference constantly throws up new issues which are explored in order to help the pupils become better writers. These issues also help to sustain the teacher's growing experience of the writing process. Over time the teacher begins to anticipate the common ones and has strategies for supporting the children effectively. There follows a brief description of some of the issues that teachers may encounter.

Writing blocks affect most children at some time during writing workshop. A common problem can be finding an initial idea for the text. As I described above, a brainstorm can support many children stuck for an idea. Children also get blocks in the middle of a piece of writing: 'I don't know what to write next.' Teachers need to evaluate exactly how much support they should give the child. For some children this may be as direct as actually suggesting the next sentence or piece of action; for others this involves pushing them to use their own knowledge and problem solving abilities.

The issue of how pieces of writing are influenced by other texts and experiences is linked to writer's block. Many children see the use of other people's ideas as 'copying'. The teacher needs to communicate the idea that writers do not work in a vacuum. Originality is a mixture of new ideas and the adoption of old ones. Most texts should offer enough original material if they are to appeal to their readers. The problem for the teacher is conveying to the child how they can achieve this balance. For example, David was having difficulties with the progress of his writing:

'I don't know where this story is going.'
'Tell me what has happened so far.'
[David summarizes the story]
'So the first two chapters seem to be setting the scene. Then the children go into the ghost house. What happens next?'
'Well, they get attacked by a man but some of them escape.'
'Right, why don't you limit the story to five chapters? In chapter three you could have the main event where the children are attacked. In chapter four the others could get the police, and chapter five could be your ending. How does that sound?'
'Oh yeah! That's OK.'

Violence often appears in children's stories, and some may choose to write horror stories. The early fascination with ghosts and haunted houses soon becomes influenced by horror films and horror books such as the 'Point Horror' series or 'Goosebumps'. The difficulty for the teacher and pupils alike is the level of violence and how it is described. An endless stream of blood and gore does not result in a text of quality; however, violent incidents which are used sparingly and sensitively can be effective. The playground bully is a good example, where one well described bullying incident leads to rightful capture and punishment. But what if the outcome is not so positive? The text may also be effective if it represents a troubling reality. It is possible that the teacher may be given an insight into real social problems the child is encountering. The choices that children make over their writing can indicate social characteristics as well as cognitive ones.

Some young writers adopt a style which sounds like a combination of sports commentary and cartoon or comic writing. One of the positive aspects of this style of writing is its originality, bizarreness and humour. On the negative side it can seem like a stream of consciousness, but with a weak structure. If this becomes a persistent way of writing, the teacher can direct the pupil towards a better story structure with opening, characters, significant events, effective ending etc. At other times the pupil may be encouraged to read and experiment with real sports commentary scripts or comic strips.

Bilingual children often need much encouragement to use the language skills they have. It is tempting to assume that the open agenda of writing workshop would be enough to allow them to produce dual language texts and/or texts which are rooted in their experience. But the teacher usually needs to make direct suggestions to the children which show that this kind of work is valued. Often the young bilingual writer has developed English writing skills beyond their skills in the other languages and may not feel confident to offer other scripts. However, there are often people at home who can supply the Urdu script, for example. This kind of work has many benefits: the school community benefits from a wider understanding of language development, the bilingual pupils are shown that their experiences are valued, and a start is being made to forming a partnership with the family and community.

Young writers often like to use people in the class as characters in their books, including the teacher. If this is done in a positive way it can give special excitement to members of the class to see their names in books and to read about the character's exploits. A potential problem arises if the characters are not appealing to the person concerned. The teacher needs to help the pupils to understand that any real life characters need to be portrayed in a positive light or they would not agree to allow their name to be used. For older children, discussions on the concept of libel can put this into a more realistic perspective.

This selection of broad issues which I have described could easily be met by the teacher in one writing workshop session. To conclude this section on writing conference, there follows one teacher's description of her interaction one morning during writing workshop. The passage illustrates the range of demands that are made on the teacher.

David was struggling with his next chapter. I suggested that his Playdo character could go to school like Vlad the Drac had in the class reader. Helped Danny measure out the lettering for his front cover. He decided to use a style taken from the book he was reading. Carl couldn't remember how to retrieve his document from the word processor. James explained that his two characters called Mud and Mud had to remain undiscovered in his story. Lorraine wanted to know if she could write her story for younger children, we discussed the importance of audience. Bejay wanted an idea for his second chapter, I suggested that the dead body might rise out of the coffin and catch them. Tim's work was excellent, he had effectively used elements of a story he was reading (about the Moomins) for his own text. I told him I liked the language he used ('they knocked their secret knock') and we agreed that there was a similarity with Zendak's 'Where the Wild Things Are'. Corrected Daniel's spellings where the meaning was unclear. Ravi's use of the words 'hip hop music' and characters called 'Trash and Buzz' was fascinating; helped him lay out speech better. Anne couldn't think of any French names so I suggested she consult the library classification. Unfortunately nothing relevant so I suggested what I could. Gurvinda has decided that he doesn't want people to use his nickname any more so in his text he had included a character saying 'Gary?' 'No, GURVINDA!' Irma's writing was rather mundane so I asked her if she had thought about the main event that was going to happen. Thomas's characters grew to 'one, yes one metre tall'. I checked that he realised how long a metre was because he seemed to be inadvertently implying that the characters shrank. I mentioned that I thought his story had been influenced by 'Vlad the Drac'. He agreed and said that Indiana Jones was another influence. Malcolm offered a passage he particularly wanted to read:

'I'm Clark Kent from the Daily Planet.'
'You mean you're Superman!'
'Shhh.'

Sharing writing

The workshop is usually concluded with a time for sharing some of the texts in progress. This helps the children to think further about the effectiveness of their writing. Sharing time is a good opportunity to give children advice on how best to respond to a piece of writing. Just as the teacher responds to writing in a positive way, the children are taught to do the same:

1 Say something you liked about the writing.
2 Suggest one thing you would improve.

This final part of the workshop draws the session to a close and allows further examination of any issues that have arisen.

The publishing cycle

The classroom ethos during writing workshop is designed to be a microcosm of the real world of publishing. The children are encouraged to make all the decisions that professional writers do. The teacher acts as final editor for the children's work and decides when it is suitable for publication.

The process of publication may involve many stages. I have described the generation of ideas which leads to the early drafts. The early drafts lead to later writing which has been proofread to varying degrees of skill, mainly by the writer themselves, sometimes by their peers and usually by the teacher. The incentive for doing all this work is often seen as the bookmaking itself. Bookmaking equipment is available in the classroom. The front and back covers of the book need to be designed. For most work, A4 or A5 paper can be mounted on card covers; however, there is a wide range of books which use paper technology for special effects (see Johnson 1990). The books the children make can be as complex as required. I think it is important to remember that the text itself is the most important element of the book, and no matter how skilfully engineered the book is, this will not change the quality of the text. Titles can be written with italic pens, copied from Letraset catalogues or word processed. Book binding machines are the best way of fixing children's books. The plastic comb binding machines are reasonably priced and offer a professional finish to much hard work.

Once the book has been published it will usually be placed in the class reading area. This is when a whole new type of learning is involved: the writers find out how popular their books are; discussions and debates rage concerning things which the children find interesting; the literary society of the classroom begins to fashion the life the book will have once it leaves the writer's hands. This kind of learning is crucial to the language development of the classroom. The nature of this learning is very quick, child centred and wide ranging. It would be impossible for the teacher to consciously orchestrate these experiences in a meaningful way for all children.

Recording development

The writing workshop offers the teacher unrivalled opportunities to observe and reflect upon children's writing development. A good recording system fulfils a number of purposes. Primarily it tracks children's progress and allows the teacher to make informed judgements on what strategies are most appropriate. However, a good recording system also contributes to the teacher's professional development by offering insights into the art of teaching and learning. In Chapter 6 I go into more detail about the possibilities for whole school recording systems and their benefits for teachers and schools. For the teacher in the classroom a system is required which is manageable and meaningful.

Simple ticklists can be too restrictive and generally limit the possibilities for recording the subtleties and qualitative aspects of the teaching and learning process. The sensitive teacher who has detailed and rigorous observation skills will discover much about children's learning behaviour which does not comfortably fit with some of the simplistic notions of language development that exist. For these reasons I believe that observational comments are the best way of recording development. The teacher who interacts positively with the pupils has an ideal opportunity to assess and record their development during or immediately after the interaction.

There are two sides of the writing process which need recording, composition and transcription. The transcriptional aspects include spelling, punctuation, handwriting, presentation etc; traditionally, primary teachers have been knowledgeable about these skills. The more difficult side is compositional development. It is important that teachers support and record their children's development in written composition. In Chapter 3 I describe in more detail some aspects of composition and how teachers can learn to conceptualize this area.

The beginning of this process can include written comments on children's early drafts. If the comments that teachers make balance positive statements with constructive criticism – and if they are specific – these comments can be collated and used as a developing picture of the child's writing. This process can be formalized by using labels stuck onto the child's writing folder. Graves (1983) suggests a range of different labels that can be stuck onto the child's folder. Significantly, he involves the child in that process. What follows is an example of a label that one school used to collect observations.

At the end of a writing conference with the child, the teacher decides whether to make a written observation on the child's writing in progress, their current development or the nature of the interaction that has just taken place. The observation is written down in the appropriate column and dated.

Table 1.1 Format for recording observations about writing

Composition	Transcription

Teacher: I liked the beginning and the middle section of your story, but I'm not sure about your ending. What do you think?
Child: I don't know. Maybe it ends too quickly.
Teacher: It is a short story, but that can be OK. What about if you removed this last sentence? I think the second to last one ended the story really well.
Child: OK.
[Teacher puts a line through the last sentence. Child seems happier now.]
Can I start on my front cover now, because when I finish this book I am going to do a book about gems?
Teacher: Of course you can.

Had the interaction followed the course of the example above, the teacher could have made the following comment: 'Darren used some imaginative language in his first story. He thought the ending was rather short. Helped him to think about the ending.' This would be recorded in the composition column and dated. Throughout the year these comments help to build up a detailed picture of the children's development and offer the possibility for further analysis to aid future teaching.

The first section of this chapter has outlined the practical elements of the writing workshop. In the second half I turn to examples of children's texts produced under these conditions. Each text illuminates information about the pupil concerned and the way the teacher worked with that pupil. The texts also serve to raise further issues which teachers encounter during writing workshop.

Children and texts

Range

One of the major advantages of writing workshop is the increased range of texts which the children can offer. This contrasts with the results obtained by setting a writing task which all the children have to carry out. The difference is the possibility of 30 different texts as opposed to 30 variations on one text. Both approaches have their place, and the most appropriate teaching must surely use both. One can explore a particular form in more detail if all the pupils are experimenting with it, and the knowledge and skills needed to use the form effectively can be quickly passed around the class. However, writing workshop does offer a unique advantage to find out what the children's interests are and their level of development.

By looking at the range of writing that children choose, teachers can assess the nature of that range for individual children and for the class as a whole. During the mini-lesson at the start of a writing workshop a class were asked by the teacher to describe the piece of writing they were working on. The following is a list of the children's ideas, giving a contextual background pointing to the origin of the idea and an indication of the nature of teacher support given during writing conference.

- *Computer games and how to cheat*
  The two pupils came up with the idea. The teacher suggested a survey of other children in the school who might be able to offer ways of getting through the levels on computer games. The teacher also suggested a format which would serve as a framework for the writing about each game.
- *A book of patterns*
  Self-generated idea with the teacher offering guidance on the amount of text that would be required and the nature of that text.
- *Tools mania*
  A flair for practical design technology projects resulted in one of the pair of pupils choosing this topic, which involved writing a manual for the use of tools. Both pupils found the necessary expository writing a challenge.
- *The new girl*
  The girl herself was new to the school, and this title may have provided her with a means of exploring some of her own feeling when she first arrived.
- *Manchester United fanzine*
  This was a particularly welcome project, as it involved three girls working on an interest they had in football. It was an opportunity to challenge the stereotypes connected with football. The teacher set a strict deadline, as the project seemed to be growing too big, and also suggested that the girls send the finished magazine to the football club to see what they thought.
- *Football story*
  The pupil worked unaided, only requesting the teacher's support to check transcription.
- *A book of children's games*
  Using a book from home, the pupil chose her favourite games and transcribed them in her own words.
- *Secret messages*
  Various secret messages which the reader had to work out were included in the book. This was aimed at the younger children and involved a series of descriptions of unknown objects which the reader had to find around the school.
- *Kitten for Nicole*
  This was an advanced piece of narrative; the teacher made minor suggestions for improving the ending. Unfortunately the child decided she didn't like the text and started on a new one without publishing this.

- *Book for young children*
  The two boys used pop art-style cartoons for the illustrations as a means of appealing to the younger children. The teacher gave some input on the kinds of material that were likely to appeal to the younger children. One of the pair tended to let the other do most of the work, and the teacher encouraged the sharing out of tasks.
- *Football magazine*
  There had been an epidemic of football magazines and the teacher made a decision that this was to be the last one for a time in order to ensure a balance of forms. The two boys used ideas from various professional magazines, combining photographs with their own text.
- *Information about trains*
  Great interest in one of the school's information books, which included impressive pull-out sections, was the stimulus for this text. At the time the work in progress consisted of a large drawing of a train. The teacher had concerns that concentration on the drawing could become a strategy for avoiding writing.
- *The magic coat*
  An expertly presented dual language story which had been written with help from the child's mother for the Urdu script. The home computer had also been used to create borders and titles. The teacher's role simply involved taking an interest in the progress.
- *Catchphrase*
  Pupil's doodling had given the teacher an idea for an activity which involved devising catchphrases based on the television programme. This pupil decided to compile a book of her own catchphrases.
- *Chinwag*
  Originally two pupils had been encouraged to devise and sell a school magazine. This included market research around the school, design, word processing, editing other children's contributions, selling, accounting etc. This was a large-scale project and the original editors felt they would like to delegate the responsibility for the second issue to someone else, so two new editors took over.
- *Newspaper*
  The idea came from the two pupils, but coincided fortuitously with a competition organized by the local paper encouraging students to design their own paper. The children asked various people around the school to offer stories. Layout became an important issue. The children brought in their own camera and took pictures to illustrate their text. BBC and Acorn computers were both used, necessitating understanding of two different word processors.
- *Modern fairy tale*
  The two pupils were struggling for an idea so the teacher suggested they contact another school to find out the kinds of books they liked, with a view to writing one for them. The school was in a deprived area and had many more bilingual children than the two pupils were used to. They realized that their initial questionnaire would need modification if it was to be used again. The children at the other school expressed a preference for traditional

stories, so the two pupils decided to write a modern fairy tale. They were encouraged by the teacher to ask the opinion of bilingual peers on suitable subject matter, and for some information about India.

- *Joke book*
  The two pupils surveyed the children in the school for good jokes. This was a popular title and had been done before in the course of the year.
- *Knightrider*
  A book based on the favourite television programme of the pupil.

It can be seen from this list that the children are involved in a large range of ideas and formats. Many of the ideas are firmly rooted in the children's interests and culture, and the texts were written contemporaneously. A significant percentage of the texts involved children collaborating in twos or threes as well as those children who wrote individually. The teacher had found that groups of more than three often resulted in one of the children not being suitably involved. The children sometimes found it difficult to assign appropriate tasks to the members of the group. The flexibility of the workshop allowed for a range of groupings that were influenced by the piece of writing concerned and the children's social needs. This organization also reflected the nature of language and literacy as a social phenomenon.

Writing workshop offers the potential for a much greater range of texts which are created using the children's intrinsic motivation. Another major benefit is the opportunity for study in depth over a long period of time. Set written tasks often have a deadline; too often, this can be to start and finish on the same day. With writing workshop the session is timetabled and the children decide on the task. This means that the children are thinking about their writing prior to the day itself. Often, they will be working on texts at home which they bring in to continue. Having the time to continue with a text for as long as it takes is an important principle. The result can be texts which are longer and written with more thought.

Khalid: children's natural language

In the early years, teachers will often act as scribe for their children's compositions. This may be done by writing alongside the child's marks or by asking the child to dictate. This has the advantage of freeing the child from the constraints of transcription. The teacher has to decide whether to use the exact language of the child or to translate into more standard forms. I would argue that the writing workshop is a time when children's own language should be valued, by transcribing as closely to the original as possible. This strategy enables the teacher to reflect on the child's language development which is evident from their texts. It allows for truly differentiated interaction suitable for each child's individual needs.

Khalid arrived at the school with special needs related to his behaviour. In part these had been caused by his relationship with a twin brother who had been moved to stay with family in another part of the country. He responded enthusiastically to the writing workshop and his behaviour was much improved in the sessions. Little booklets were available for the children for early drafts. Khalid wrote the first draft and his teacher scribed onto a separate sheet, and redrafted on computer for him to arrange the text and add the illustrations. Each line below represents a different page.

The Aeroplane Flying – Written by Khalid
The stone is picking the car up and the car's key.
Then the lollipop man didn't have his lolly.
The clown is happy and he changed into the pattern.
The teddy's really skinny.
Little bit stones left. He was chucking stones. Then the star shines.
The lollipop man is waiting. Some people are waiting for their school.
Some have already gone.

By using Khalid's own language it was possible to reflect on the developing aspects of his composition. The story features the familiar figure of the lollipop man at the beginning and the end. The stones also link the early part of the story with the end. These examples help to show how Khalid is developing the idea of narrative as a continuous entity; however, he tends to have a series of pages with pictures which are loosely related. This idea is supported by the unusual title, which seems only to be related through the description of different kinds of transport. The idea of 'title' is an important concept and takes time for some young writers to develop.

Matthew: originality

Giving children control over their writing enables the teacher to evaluate the quality of their ideas for texts. Sometimes excellent presentation can mask weak ideas; at other times the originality of ideas can be marred by poor presentation. Quality of ideas is a difficult concept to assess and teach; inevitably it is partly a subjective decision on the part of the reader. However, the extent to which the pupil relies on other texts, and the way these influences are used, affects the originality of the piece. Most importantly, writing workshop ensures that such discussions take place at all.

Matthew was a quiet child who tended not to volunteer information in discussions. He seemed to be uncomfortable at times when expected to talk to staff. During writing workshop he became involved in the writing of a text which characterized a nation of peas. He was influenced by the style of comics, video games and cartoon characters, which were a consuming interest of his. The teacher encouraged his original ideas and fantasy world and worked hard at improving Matthew's presentation skills.

Peabites Enemys [*sic*]
by Matthew, Adam, Richard and James

Chapter One
It was night time in pealand when a new planet was on the monitor. They looked at the pea book of planets. The boss of the beans was bean bite. He was very strong. The peas got Pea Bite Ninja Nut and pea warriors went to fight the beans. Peas were beamed up to Beanland. It was a big fight.

Often it is possible for the teacher to recognize the variety of influences which children use in their texts. This is important because it helps teachers to be more aware of the cultural and social aspects which affect their pupils' lives, enabling their teaching to be more relevant to the pupils' immediate needs. However, in this example the teacher was interested by the originality and bizarreness of pealand but didn't find any specific influence other than the child's imagination and the 'Ninja Turtles' who were popular at the time.

Lawrence: sequels, stereotypes and prolificacy

The writing workshop gives time for children to develop ideas to a natural conclusion. Sometimes that conclusion may be the waste bin, but most of the time the result is a text which has been given their full involvement. Having come up with a good idea and published the result, the question is what to do next. For some children the obvious idea is a sequel. The flexibility of the writing workshop allows this possibility. The difficulties usually associated with how long children must write for and knowing when something is finished are greatly alleviated, as many pieces can be in progress and children can have infinitely varied start and finish times.

Lawrence was a confident child who had a particular aptitude for mathematics. He found the composition side of writing problematic. His solution to this problem was to write about the things that motivated him, so he started with his passion for football. In spite of much help with redrafting both for composition and transcription, Lawrence's teacher felt that he had not succeeded in changing Lawrence's belief that the first draft was the most important.

Fantastic Football

. . . The next day we played in the quarter finals we won 3–0. That match was easy the next match was against FC Barcelona. Ian got fowled the other player got a yellow card [picture of card]. The ref said 'one more of them sonny and you'll be off'. It was a penalty who was going to take it? It was Simon with 1 minute left he's running up and boot yes its in.

The teacher was able to monitor the choice of topics in relation to gender. Aware of the work of CLPE (the Centre for Language in Primary Education) on gender and reading (Barrs and Pidgeon 1993) which suggested that boys tended to have a preference for non-fiction, she was able to compare these findings with her own work. It was clear to the teacher that a significant number of boys liked to write stories. This was not a simple contradiction of the findings of CLPE. Reading their stories carefully revealed that the language was influenced by football reporting in the press and football commentary generally; both these forms are described as non-fiction, and their influence was strong on Lawrence's story. This point also illustrated the complexities of genre. The child's writing development emerged within the combination of different spoken and written genres.

Lawrence's preference for sequel revealed itself on the back page of one of his books.

(If you are a football freak you should read this book)
(read football at flixton then football at flixton 2 then you may read this book about flixton football team playing different clubs)

He became a prolific writer, publishing many books. Often he preferred the publishing to the hard work required in meaningful redrafting. This preference even stretched to writing sequels for other children's books. Sally had written *Halloween I*, so Lawrence asked if he could write the sequel.

Halloween II

Chapter I
We could hear faint tapping noises. It came louder and louder and even louder until a small hole came in the ground. It was Lorraine she said 'what are you waiting for come on.' Collette went down first then Shona then Jack then me. All of a sudden a jail guard came we ran hell for leather and soon we were out of the remand home.

Lawrence's teacher felt that the quality of his composition had improved and we see this from the two extracts. Apart from the direct teaching involved, the opportunity to publish many texts and to extend the work of other children contributed to Lawrence's development.

Kirsty: writing in depth

Stories play an important part in writing workshop. Children often choose story above other forms because stories are a natural motivator, and the creation of imaginary worlds is important for their general development. Stories are part of the human desire to celebrate life and to better understand personal experiences . . . a key way to make sense of our lives. Partly because of this, teachers often set tasks involving story writing (Barrs 1990; White 1989). The role of story is particularly important for younger children, but at Key Stage 2 story still has an important role to play. Writing development can occur not just by experiencing a wide range of written genres, but also by practising and refining one particular form repeatedly.

When considering the development of writing there has been a strong argument to suggest that even the youngest children should be exposed to a wide range of genres. It is important that children's writing opportunities are not just limited to story writing and the weekly diary. However, it is possible that at different times during the development of writing, certain genres should be emphasized more than others according to the children's developing interests. For example, children as young as two delight in the listening, remembering and singing of nursery rhymes. This can dominate all other genres for a period of time. The parent or teacher should surely celebrate and extend this enthusiasm and learning rather than try to enforce a wider range of genres at that time.

Kirsty was a reserved child who started the year not enjoying writing. She was competent and above the national average for most subjects, but lacked any real motivation to write. By the end of the year her mother, who was also a teacher, commented, 'Kirsty used to hate writing but now she can't get enough of it. I wish I could get the kids in my class to enjoy writing so much!'

Most of Kirsty's writing workshops during one year were taken up with the writing of two texts. The first was a story book called *Teddy's Adventure in London*. The book ended up as 31 pages of A5 text. The opening of the story was as follows:

> Danielle Hall was going to stay with her Grandma in London. Danielle was a little girl seven years old, with black hair and brown eyes. She went on a plane and a bus. Grandma was standing outside when she saw Danielle coming on the bus. She ran as fast as she could to the bus stop. Danielle got off the bus and kissed her grandma then they went back to the house. Grandma went to make tea and Danielle went to unpack her things. When she got bored Grandma gave her some money so she went to the corner shop. It took her a quarter of an hour to choose but she got a teddy bear in the end. Then she went back for her lunch. They had pea and ham soup. Grandma said to Danielle
> 'Why did you eat all the bread and butter?'
> Danielle said 'I didn't but Grandma couldn't it have been teddy?'
> 'No Danielle don't be silly teddies can't eat.'
> Danielle said 'It could be a magic teddy!'
> Grandma was going to say go and get ready for bed when Danielle came down ready for bed. So her Grandma just kissed her and she fell asleep.
> But you know what was going to happen and so does teddy.

Kirsty sets the scene expertly and offers a good introduction to her story. It nicely explores aspects of the relationship between children and their grandmas and implies some of the causes and effects for their behaviour. The extract was written as Chapter 1 and contains a skilful final sentence which invites the reader into the world of the writer and offers a cliffhanger to tempt us to read on. The device of using the narrator to ask the reader questions was used throughout the story.

Each chapter of the story contained an event for Teddy and Danielle. In Chapter 2 they go to the cinema to see *Home Alone 2*.

> Teddy's best bit was where the lady pushed the kidnappers over with her bag. Danielle's best bit was when the kidnapper fell on the marbles.

Teddy's character is gradually developed and we see that he has different views from Danielle about the film. In Chapter 3 he escapes into a museum which has 'all people dressed in old clothes'. For the first time Teddy speaks:

> Teddy said to himself 'I better not move in case someone sees me. But how can I get back to Danielle in time?'

Part of the appeal of the story is the mystery element that is included. Is Teddy really alive?

> Danielle was thinking Teddy had ate the popcorn because it wasn't there. When she looked at the peanut butter it had gone, so it was Teddy.

Chapter 5 has the classic teddy bear activity:

> Joe and Danielle were playing with their best teddy when Danielle said 'let's make a Teddy bear picnic.'

In Chapters 5 and 6 Kirsty introduced some of the issues that were part of her thinking and related to the process of her growing up. Boyfriends, girlfriends and discos become part of Teddy's exploits.

> Annabel had already got a boyfriend but she was starting to like teddy because of the jokes he was telling her [. . . .] Annabel's boyfriend was on side. His name was James, he looked big and strong so teddy wasn't going to mess with him.
>   Danielle and Joe had gone to bed. But can you remember when Annabel was talking to Teddy before the picnic, she had said to teddy 'would you like to come to my party we are having a disco on the dining room table?'

The story structure was helped by Kirsty's decision to choose Danielle's trip to her grandma's as a natural duration for the text. However, even the ending – which basically involves Danielle returning home – contains an extra dimension in its description of feelings.

> Danielle got up and thought about going home. She didn't want to go home because she liked Joe and Grandma better than some people that she knew.

This teacher's role in this text was mainly to discuss elements of the overall structure. Kirsty found it quite hard to keep the idea of the whole story in mind, although she managed to avoid repetition very successfully. The teacher also had difficulty during writing conference because of the length of the text. It became necessary to read the story over non-contact times and make a series of written comments to help Kirsty redraft certain sections rather than cover the feedback during writing conference.

The remainder of Kirsty's writing workshop during the year was taken up by a selection of short plays called Teddy's Plays. The use of the first piece of fiction as the influence for a series of plays was unusual. Without the classroom organization of the writing workshop, this individual achievement probably would not have arisen. The higher order thinking skills involved in the manipulation and control of such long texts are a direct benefit of the writing workshop.

Writing workshop is a central part of the process approach to writing. It offers pupils the opportunity to develop as real writers within a publishing cycle which is initiated in the classroom. It offers teachers the experience of learning a great deal more about their pupils and about themselves as teachers.

TWO

Emergent writing

During the early years of education the process approach is encouraged through the practices and philosophies of emergent writing. Teaching through emergent writing builds on the language and literacy experience that the child has gained prior to coming to school. Many studies have shown that most children learn a large amount about language and literacy before they enter the nursery or reception class. It would be illogical to start them all from the same baseline, and so the approach attempts to give the opportunity for children to demonstrate what they have learned, and for teaching to take that learning as a starting point.

If teachers are to find out what children have learned about writing, an approach needs to be taken that encourages the children to write from day one. Nursery and reception children are often keen to show what they can do, and their attempts at writing give a clear indication to the teacher of their stage of development. Having observed the children's writing behaviour, the teacher is in a better position to decide the kind of experiences and activities that the children will need to extend their development.

In the course of this chapter I first look at the classroom organization that supports emergent writing; this section identifies some of the main practical features of the approach. This is followed by reflections on some of the theories that underpin emergent literacy. The links between emergent writing and writing workshop are briefly examined in order to show that emergent writing can be a natural starting point for the development of writing work-shop. The chapter concludes by identifying possible ways forward for the practice of emergent writing, and these points are linked with comments from two teachers who have significant experience of this kind of teaching.

Classroom organization

The 'writing area' is designed to motivate the children to write in an area where all the possible resources that they may need are ready to hand. The area is clearly labelled as a writing area, and with the reading area, listening area and role play area, makes up the language space of the classroom. The furniture in the area is organized so that children can work in small groups or pairs. Usually the area will contain no more than eight places; screens can be used to divide the area when appropriate, and these offer further display space for the children's writing. The teacher encourages the children to work regularly in the writing area. Although the teacher creates an expectation that the children will regularly work in the area, the choice over what to write is offered to the children.

The horizontal and vertical display spaces offer the opportunity to display a range of texts. Children's work is displayed; some of this will be redrafted standard English, some will be the children's writing unaltered, and other writing may have the teacher's writing alongside explaining the meaning to other readers. In order to encourage a range of writing, a variety of texts are displayed including environmental print and different languages. In addition, teaching aids including alphabet friezes, word collections, rules/conventions for writing etc can all form part of these displays.

Although teachers control much of the organization and display of writing, the children can sometimes be involved in their own organization. Message boards provide a useful stimulus where children are given complete control over their own board. Often this results in many pictures that reflect the peer group culture. The purpose of a message board is of course to pass on messages. Children do this all the time orally and may not see the relevance of a message board; however, teachers can put up their own messages to stimulate writing. For example, 'I don't think that any children in this class should have stayed up to watch *Batman*! Write what *you* think.'

A range of resources are supplied that are easily accessible, easy to tidy, labelled and meticulously stored. This can enhance the physical appearance of the area and gives children the resources they may want to use for their writing. The resources include standard pencils, coloured pencils, felt pens, crayons, rulers, rubbers, cheap paper for initial drafts, a range of coloured paper, better quality paper for final drafts, lined paper, bookmaking card, staplers, hole punches, string, glue, scissors, prepared booklets of differing page lengths, line guides, lettering catalogues, dictionaries etc. Bookmaking equipment is an important aspect of this provision.

Role-play areas are set up to maximize the possibilities for language and literacy learning. The scope for these is endless, but teachers have successfully set up hospitals, travel agents, builders' merchants, shops, market stalls, electrical repair shops etc. The office as a role-play area is often successful because it uses resources that suggest communication. Telephones, for example, give children a natural resource that stimulates oracy and the role-play of people talking at work; phone message pads extend this process. Typewriters and computers motivate children to produce new texts. Forms to fill in and letters to post extend the range of written forms.

The children are encouraged to act like experienced writers from day one in the nursery. In order to do this they must feel confident to take risks, and know that mistakes will be seen as a necessary part of their development: the notions of mark-making and invented spelling are important ones. If children are prepared to 'have a go' at their spelling this allows the teacher to be more selective with their interaction. Once this confidence to invent spellings is established, the teacher begins the process of helping the children towards standard spelling. All the time a balance is struck between the expectation that children progress towards standard forms and the concern that an over-emphasis on standard spelling can inhibit the child's composition. In a minority of cases this inhibition results in the child feeling unable to put any words on paper. At the other end of the spectrum there are children who continue to invent spellings for too long and who need specific intervention in order to develop their phonetic and visual spelling strategies.

Work in the writing area and role-play area complements other language and literacy tasks that the teacher delivers. The writing that the children do in these areas gives the teacher the chance to observe the children and make decisions on the kinds of structured activity they will need. These decisions are based on common problems that the children experience with their writing and the future development that the teacher expects. Sometimes the resource implications mean that experience with a particular form of writing is easier to organize as a set activity. For example, envelopes and letter writing can be very popular with children, but if envelopes are permanently available in the writing area it can be prohibitively expensive. One option is to supply envelope templates and teach the children how to make their own when required. Similarly, the design and making of greetings cards is popular but the expense of card means that this is often better as a set activity.

Whole class sessions such as writing workshops are usually more suitable for older children; however, the practice outlined in Chapter 1 can be modified for infant children. The sessions will generally be much shorter, perhaps between 15 minutes and half an hour. However, the children are still encouraged to take part in a whole class writing workshop. One teacher found that a daily morning writing session where each child had their own notebook provided an interesting record of the kind of writing they chose to do first thing each morning and a record of their developing secretarial skills. Another teacher of early years children found that by setting out different coloured paper and pencils at the tables, the children came straight in after dinner and involved themselves in writing. Both these approaches offered the children the opportunity of a first draft and possible future ideas for writing to be continued in the writing area.

One way in which teachers can structure the children's output is by setting targets for the minimum number of books they would like the child to complete by a certain time. This kind of global structuring occurs in many different ways in the practice of emergent literacy. For some children teachers may specify the number of sentences or lines that they want the child to complete. The kind of structure that is applied is more like the kinds of demand that adult writers might face, the demands that become part of the process, such as deadlines, required number of words/pages, publishing routines, editorial input, target setting, collaborative proofreading, planning techniques, audience awareness, time spent writing etc. This kind of structure contrasts with the structure that is enforced if, for example, children are expected to copy ten spellings or write the story of Cinderella.

When responding to and assessing children's writing the teacher needs to look below the surface. With emergent writing that has been written in the writing area or role-play area, the children are able to focus on the meaning. Often the presentational aspects seem to be neglected, and yet the children show great excitement for their pieces of writing and books they have made. The teacher's desire to improve the secretarial aspects can sometimes mean that they may overlook interesting compositional aspects of the text. Conversely, some pieces of writing can be beautifully presented but the composition can be weak. Part of the answer to this problem lies in the teacher separating the two areas. With older children this separation is encouraged through a series of drafts, where initial drafts concentrate on composition and later drafts deal with transcription. In the early years the concept of redrafting is usually at an early stage of development, and typically occurs orally as the teacher is sharing the piece of writing. Much of this interaction naturally focuses on meaning and composition. To balance the emphasis on composition, the teacher sets up directed tasks that can focus more directly on presentational and secretarial aspects. For example, some excellent work has been done on 'book technology' where all kinds of unusual book formats can encourage motivation and a focus on the product. These include lift-the-flap books, zigzag books, pop-up books etc. This work on presentation filters into the work done in the writing area, and the two forms of organization support each other.

When responding to emergent writing the teacher will have a number of conflicting priorities. First and foremost the teacher ensures that the child's motivation to write is maintained. Over the first few weeks of the year expectations and routines are established. The children soon realize the control they are being offered, and they begin to experiment and enjoy the relative freedom of emergent writing. As the teacher develops relationships with the individual children, they know the kind of feedback that will be most productive. Very often the teacher will comment on an aspect of the piece of writing that they enjoyed or found interesting. Sometimes they may ask a question about something of genuine interest to them, something about the piece of writing that caused them to reflect. Often the teacher will want to comment on the secretarial aspects of the text. They encourage the child to read the writing again and to try and notice things that need to be changed.

The teacher can also experience conflicting feelings for work that is finished and that is ready for display or presentation. Societal expectations to present standard English may conflict with the teacher's ability to recognize high quality work at an early stage of development. There should always be times when children's original work is displayed and valued as it is. This will mean that it may not look like writing to some people and may contain transcription errors. There will also be times when the teacher may want to correct the work and/or ask the child to redraft it. For young children involved in book-making, the assembly of text that the teacher has transcribed, and the subsequent decisions on page organization, can involve many useful literacy lessons through this process of supported redrafting.

With young writers the teacher will often write sections of the text again in standard English so that the child can compare the two versions. This may be done on a separate piece of paper if the teacher does not want to spoil the child's work. Sometimes it may be written underneath to provide an easier comparison. Many lessons are possible at this point: for example, if the text is rewritten onto card the individual words can be cut up and re-assembled. As the child learns one-to-one correspondence, the understanding of the concept of 'word' can take much of the teacher's time. Some teachers occasionally offer circles that the child is expected to write each word in. At other times the child is encouraged to listen to their own spoken words and segment them. This is aimed to show that speech and writing have important differences: speech is offered in units of information and is structured according to the shared needs of the people involved in the dialogue; writing is structured in words and sentences and occurs without immediate feedback from the intended audience. The understanding of the concepts of word and sentence is not straightforward and can take much time and effort on the part of teachers and children.

Shared writing involves the teacher acting as scribe for pair or group compositions. The group of children offer suggestions for the writing of a text which the teacher writes on a flipchart or board. This technique frees the children from the constraints of transcription and enables them to expand their compositional thinking. Having written the first draft of such a piece collaboratively, the children are then encouraged to write their own text. Sometimes this may be along the same lines as the shared writing. At other times children will be encouraged to extend this and use their own ideas.

The idea of teacher as scribe in a one-to-one situation is a useful strategy for lifting the constraints of transcription if the child is particularly lacking in confidence. Most children should be able to write freely once the classroom ethos has been established; however, there will often be a minority of children who struggle to get ideas on paper. Occasionally the teacher may scribe a complete piece for the child. At other times they may recommend the use of the tape recorder or recommend that another child could help. The teacher is constantly looking to improve the child's independence and pass control of the writing back to the child. If the teacher writes the opening sentence they will be wanting the child to write the second sentence. If they offer some ideas for the introduction they will want the child to carry through the middle and end, and so on. Some children may benefit from the chance to copy certain sections. Copying or 'copywriting' is sometimes used as a major component in the teaching of writing. It is important that teachers rationalize the benefits and potential problems with copying. When used appropriately, copying can help with letter formation and the memory of certain words; it can also support the presentational skills. If copying is used too much it restricts the child's independence and impedes their compositional development.

There is much evidence that children develop reading and writing through environmental print. Studies have shown that children's awareness of print in the environment starts very young. For example, in the home, children as young as two become curious about shopping lists and food labelling, and parents interact with their children in order to develop their knowledge. In order to build on that knowledge, teachers have used environmental print as a stimulus for activities in the classroom. Sometimes this is through structured tasks such as matching the taste of different crisps to their original packets, leading into crisp packet design and possibly a shop selling the different designs. At other times it reflects the teacher's practice of filling the classroom with purposeful, attractive and interactive displays of print.

Response journals can be another interesting facet of emergent writing. They encapsulate the ideals of teacher response to writing, particularly with respect to composition. The children each have a book that is their journal. This differs from a traditional diary writing task in that the teacher responds to the writing by asking written questions and making written statements. These questions and statements encourage the children to extend their writing and provide further information about the text and the events portrayed. The process is time consuming, as the teacher has many responses to write, so it is often best restricted to a set period, perhaps half a term. Often the writing has a special expressive quality that is well worth sharing by reading aloud to the class or publishing as a class anthology, provided the entries are not intended to be private.

When children are given the freedom to write and an ethos is created that encourages originality, the particular character of emergent writing often excites teachers. Gundlach (1981: 143) saw this writing as 'compressed and, sometimes, elliptical'. The relatively open framework of emergent writing allows the teacher to continue to see glimpses of writing that inspire genuine interest. The teacher's enthusiasm is vital for maintaining the children's motivation, and this response is, of course, personal. Yet over time teachers have found that they find recurring themes of interest in the children's emergent writing. The following examples illustrate particular extracts that one teacher found in her bilingual children's writing that caused her to reflect. The children were aged from five to seven.

'Mr Lowlo.
He was scared. Then when he screamed his hair went up.'
I was interested in Yasif's choice of title because he had used his own mispronunciation of a teacher's name as the basis for a character in his book. I thought the image of Mr Lowlo's hair going up was particularly visual and perhaps was inspired by cartoons.

'He knocked at the house. The giant said "mmm, I got you for my dinner."
The boy says "Please don't eat me!"
"OK"'
I liked the way Nina had included elements of traditional stories in her own book. I wondered how important the oral story telling tradition was to the children. The way the giant tricks the boy was funny; Raymond Briggs perhaps.

'Why always girls cry? Why always boys kick the girls? All of us cry.'
This expression of feelings and a common complaint was unusual because it was expressed in question form within a 'story'. I wondered if the final sentence was a reflection on the implications for all the children in the class.

'If you break my window I'm going to lock you up in a cage.'
I thought that Andrew had combined the modern problem of vandalism with the kind of response that Hansel faced. At the time this kind of consequential statement was unusual.

I have identified some of the major features of emergent writing in the classroom. These features are underpinned by the central philosophy that makes a positive assumption about children's ability to learn. This philosophy is supported by research that has looked at the development of writing prior to formal schooling.

Theory and research

The term 'emergent literacy' was popularized by Hall (1987) in his book *The Emergence of Literacy*. Over time, emergent literacy in the classroom has become particularly related to emergent writing. The basis of the philosophy is the notion of the child as an active and motivated learner who experiments with a wide range of written forms out of a sense of curiosity and a desire to learn. Hall described emergent literacy as follows:

> It implies that development takes place from within the child . . . 'emergence' is a gradual process. For something to emerge there has to be something there in the first place. Where emergent literacy is concerned this means the fundamental abilities children have, and use, to make sense of the world . . . things usually only emerge if the conditions are right. Where emergent literacy is concerned that means in contexts which support, facilitate enquiry, respect performance and provide opportunities for engagement in real literacy acts.
>
> (Hall 1987: 9)

There has been criticism that this kind of approach encourages teachers to be 'non-teachers' and that it does not involve direct instruction. The approach is certainly rather more subtle than the idea that children enter school as empty vessels ready to be filled with knowledge and skills. One of its features is that it builds on children's motivation through the implicit positiveness of the theories. Children are assumed to already have many of the fledgling understandings that will enable the teacher to build on these and develop experienced language users. It also implies that the teacher looks carefully to find exactly what the child can do before they assume what the child cannot do. By organizing open-ended learning opportunities that enable the teacher to observe and find the optimum level at which to pitch the teaching, the teacher is ideally placed to offer direct instruction when appropriate. The teacher recognizes that there are times when the ability to stand back and *not* intervene can do the child more good than the unremitting direct instruction and ill thought out intervention which are common in some classrooms. Again the issue is one of balance, and it is impossible to prescribe a particular percentage of direct instruction versus facilitation and encouragement. This balance is closely tied to the particular relationship between teacher and individual pupil.

The concept of emergent writing is very closely linked with the practice of developmental writing; in fact it is very difficult to draw distinctions between the two. The following list identifies some of the key features of developmental writing and was influenced by Browne's (1993: 21) points that characterize such writing:

1 Builds on children's literacy experience prior to coming to school.
2 Encourages independent writing from day one of the nursery.
3 Modelling is provided by physical resources and the actions of the teacher.
4 Transcription errors are dealt with after the meaning has been established. A smaller number of errors are corrected, but each one in more detail.
5 Learning to write developmentally can be slow, but the benefits in future motivation for writing are the result.
6 Writing tasks emphasize purpose and real reasons.
7 Children have time to develop pieces of writing in depth.
8 The confidence to take risks is encouraged.

The National Writing Project (1989) reported that some teachers expressed concerns about aspects of developmental writing. These concerns particularly focused on children who felt inhibited. Because they did not feel confident to take risks and use invented spellings they struggled to get ideas down on paper. It was suggested that these children need to be offered a range of strategies that enable them to develop their confidence. Sometimes a relatively private notebook where children can express ideas, feelings and thoughts can help. For others a picture planning approach can help; for example, fold a piece of paper into sections and draw a picture for each section, then have a go at writing a sentence for each picture. Sometimes if even the relative freedom of invented spelling is inhibitive the child can be encouraged to use a 'spelling line' where any unknown letters are replaced by a line. This helps the child move on to the next word without dwelling for too long on the previous one.

There can be no doubt that children learn a vast amount about language and literacy prior to entering the nursery. There is a large research base that indicates that this position is true. The research ranges from in-depth studies of individual children (Bissex 1980; Payton 1984; Laycock 1990) to studies of larger groups (Ferreiro and Teberosky 1982; Harste *et al.* 1984; Tizard and Hughes 1984; Wells 1986). Many of these studies emphasize the richness and quality of the learning that is evident in the home. Teachers who are unaware of such research findings may make negative assumptions about children entering school for the first time: 'these children have no language', 'children from poorer homes can't learn much because they don't have many books'. These kinds of assumption lead directly to low expectations of what the children might achieve. Teachers pitch their level of teaching at the lowest common denominator, which gives no opportunity for the children to demonstrate what they really can do.

Of the studies mentioned above, Harste *et al.*'s (1984) award winning American work is perhaps the most challenging. They investigated the language and literacy experiences of sixty-eight 3 to 6-year-olds. Their evidence is an overwhelming testimony to the achievements of these children. Like Tizard and Hughes, they found scant evidence that children from economically poor homes necessarily learned significantly less about language and literacy. Their conclusions raised some disturbing questions about traditional approaches to language and literacy. In one of the chapters in *Language Stories and Literacy Lessons* Harste *et al.* give a detailed account of the experiences of a 6-year-old called Alison. They reached the following conclusion:

> Data collected from Alison and some sixty-seven other 3-, 4-, 5-, and 6-year-olds (Harste, Burke, Woodward 1981, 1983) leads us to conclude that many of the instructional assumptions currently made by teachers are faulty at best and debilitating at worst. In no instance – and our data have been collected from boys and girls in high, middle, and low SES, black and white, small town and urban inner-city families – would the assumptions underlying Alison's instruction have been appropriate ones from which to operate instructionally.
>
> (Harste *et al.* 1984: 14)

Harste *et al.* found that the formal language teaching that was going on in the schools was based on questionable assumptions about children's early development. A lack of understanding of the learning that had taken place in the home resulted in inappropriate use of formal teaching methods. The evidence does not suggest that children should be left alone to get on with their work. All the studies of the children at home illustrate the important contribution that parents, other adults and other experienced language users make in the development of language and literacy in the young child. It is their natural interaction and sometimes direct instruction that helps the children learn. Teachers must constantly look for organizational strategies that enable children to demonstrate what they know. Having found out this information it is vital that teachers are pro-active and that they use their knowledge to provide the appropriate balance of direct instruction, support and encouragement for individual children and the class as a whole.

It can be seen that the philosophies that underpin emergent writing emphasize the fact that the great majority of children are enthusiastic language learners. This positive expectation of children is based on research that has looked at their behaviour in the home and the nursery. Most importantly I suggest that we cannot ignore the voice of the child and his/her motivation when we decide how to approach writing.

The links between emergent writing and writing workshop

Clear links can be found between emergent writing and writing workshop described in Chapter 1. Table 2.1 illustrates these links.

As can be seen, there are a number of overlaps between emergent writing and writing workshop. In general the differences come down to the experience of the writers. Emergent writing is mainly focused in the early years. As the children become more experienced writers they are better equipped to understand the nature of writing workshop and its standardized organization.

Table 2.1   Comparison of emergent writing approach with writing workshop

Emergent writing	Writing workshop
• Builds on learning from home	• Encourages writing at school to be continued at home and vice versa
• Open-ended organization that encourages writing	• Encourages informed choice of genre/topic
• Takes place daily	• Whole class regular session
• Publication	• Publication
• Initial emphasis on composition	• Early drafts emphasize composition
• Mark-making encouraged	• Invented spelling
• Emphasis on learning to write	• Developing emphasis on writing to learn
• Sometimes collaborative	• Often collaborative
• Significance of teacher interaction in writing areas	• Significance of teacher interaction during writing conference
• Naturalistic recording methods	• Naturalistic recording methods
• Teacher models writing behaviour	• Teacher models writing behaviour
• Start and finish negotiated with writer	• Start and finish negotiated with writer

Emergent writing involves the teacher in understanding the kinds of experience that the child has had at home and using this knowledge to structure learning in the classroom. Similarly, the best examples of successful writing workshop involve the children in two-way learning between home and school. Ideas for writing are developed at home, sometimes they are continued during writing workshop, and at other times they progress simultaneously. Work from writing workshop is also taken home; sometimes this work is redrafted at home using a personal computer.

The encouragement to write is provided by open-ended organization. The writing area is a place where writing takes place and is often spontaneous and frequent, whereas during writing workshop children are more reflective in their choice of text based on the better understandings they have of the process. They make deliberate choices based on their wider knowledge and better understanding of genre and written forms.

The focus of emergent writing is very much on learning to write. Although this is obviously true for writing workshop as well, the emphasis shifts towards writing to learn. There are two aspects to this: the child becomes more aware of the process of writing and they are better able to reflect on some of the issues to do with writing and the writer; and they set up projects for themselves where the aim is to learn more about a particular topic of interest.

Collaboration is a feature of both approaches. In the early years this collaboration is less systematic. As children become more experienced they are helped to plan more carefully the different roles that they will fulfil when writing together. Sections of the text are allocated to different children, as are pictures and the preparation of books. Pairs of children often work well, as it is more difficult to ensure that all members of the group are occupied when three or more children are involved. However, as the collaborative skills develop, this more complex organization is possible.

Future issues for emergent writing

Discussions about emergent writing have often centred on the issue of whether to adopt the method or not. This kind of discussion sometimes results in the two sides of the argument becoming polarized, which has the effect of limiting any possible refinements of the approach. In order to continually evaluate emergent writing, teachers have to use the approach and modify it on the basis of the teaching and learning that takes place. There are a number of schools that have continued with the philosophies of emergent literacy. These schools have been able to refine the approach; in doing so they are in a position to identify issues for future practice.

In the final section of this chapter I intend to identify issues for the practice of emergent writing. In order to do this I draw on my own experience as a teacher in schools that have adopted emergent writing approaches. I also relate these issues to the transcript of an interview that I carried out with two other experienced primary teachers who have also had the opportunity to practise emergent writing over a number of years. Karen is the head teacher of an infant and nursery school. At the time of her appointment the school had practised emergent writing for some years and all the staff were committed to the approach. Prior to her appointment Karen had 16 years' teaching experience including a break to bring up her children. Gemma is the deputy head teacher of the same school; she had had several years' experience using emergent writing at the school.

Home/school partnerships

Home/school partnerships seem to be well established for reading. It is equally important that the whole school policy on writing is communicated effectively to parents. This needs to be backed up by a continuous programme, both formal and informal, that takes on board parents' thoughts about their child's writing and offers support and information. Gemma describes some of this work.

> G: It's an on-going process with each new lot of parents because they always base what their children should be doing on what happened to themselves. So for something new you've to build up their trust and show them that it works. We have found that the parents who have had a child through and who has moved to the junior school are convinced. But for those who it's their first child coming through they need taking through it.

This idea of partnership is not limited to parents. The two teachers also made the point that universities need access to schools that practise emergent writing so that newly qualified teachers are able to draw on school practice experience when they take up their first post.

Structuring emergent writing

A common criticism of emergent writing as an approach is that it lacks structure. I feel that this criticism is misplaced, but the point is important. The traditional structure for the teaching of writing is replaced by one that uses the children's predicted development as a framework for making decisions on teaching and learning. The focus is child centred rather than teacher centred. Continua are established for the development of composition and transcription, based on the experience of teaching children using emergent writing. As individual children and groups approach various milestones, the teacher's interaction and the activities they plan carry the child on to the next stage of development. Structure is often applied through directed writing time, length of text, the monitoring of the range of forms, the number of texts produced over time, activities that extend learning based on observation of children's writing behaviour etc. Structure is less often applied through decontextualized activities, formal spelling tests, copywriting, controlled vocabulary etc. However, the issue is one of balance, and emergent writing does not preclude the occasional use of these strategies if they are seen to be beneficial to a particular child. Gemma suggested that learning is enhanced if it is contextualized in the child's own writing.

> G: I think you have to have a back-up structure but rather than say diving in with the phonics, you look at something that can be developed, that's already on the paper. So if you go back to my example of the letter 'B' that I mentioned earlier, you might observe the particular piece of work and decide to look at other experiences and activities to support the understanding of 'B' sounds. So you develop the child on a more one-to-one basis as their need arises rather than 'today we are doing "B"'.

Children's motivation

Motivation is an essential aspect of successful teaching and learning. At times the motivation of the child seems to be absent from discussions on what are the most appropriate teaching methods. No approach to writing is going to be successful if the child does not enjoy writing most of the time. One of the theories behind emergent writing is that you develop more children who write for pleasure and who continue to enjoy writing once they leave school. This theory needs to be examined by schools and by researchers.

> K: At the beginning of the day, in every classroom there is a place where children can immediately go and put down their thoughts on paper. Because they are using emergent writing they can get on with it on their own and don't have to come to find the teacher to say 'Can you give me a spelling for this?' or 'how do I write this?' The teacher is then free to welcome all the children in on a very gradual basis. They come in from 8.45 in the morning. If I go into the classrooms at ten to nine, in every classroom there will be some children already

writing. They haven't needed a teacher to spark them off at all. They have just come in and wanted to do it.

The range of written forms

When children are given the choice of form the teacher is able to see the forms of writing that are important to children. Some children may develop as effective writers by an increasing sophistication with one particular form. Some may develop by regularly changing the kinds of form that they use. All children need to experience a range of forms through the set tasks that the teacher provides, but emergent writing gives an opportunity for greater specialization. This use of written forms needs to be monitored by the teacher. Karen emphasized the importance of the child seeing a purpose for different forms and the necessity to help the child identify some of the differences.

> K: For example the child has to see a reason for writing a poem. The child might not want to write a poem but if you discuss the reasons for writing poetry – for example, as a means of discussing feelings, or the way that poetry is perhaps a better vehicle for expressing feelings than story – the child may be more enthusiastic. I think you've got to be very clear on the reasons for writing. Children, if they don't have the reason for doing it, or the fun behind it, they just don't want to do it.
>
> G: I was thinking that when they are young it is often stories that you go through with young children. That's probably why they use that form of writing more readily because that's the bulk of their experience. If you are wanting children to write in a wider range you need to offer them a wider range of books earlier on, that's why the reading is tied in so much. Until you have heard it, and heard it in different forms and heard the language involved you won't start to experiment on your own . . .
>
> K: . . . and have your attention drawn to the differences, because it isn't enough just to read a non-fiction book with the children, or a story. You have actually got to get the children to say what the differences are.

The predicted rate of writing development

If the rate of development is initially slower when using emergent writing but the learning is of a higher quality, teachers need to establish patterns of development. These patterns must be used to spot those children who are not progressing as they should, and action needs to be taken to support, challenge and improve their development.

> G: I think it's slower because you're giving the child time to take it on board. I wonder if things have got a firmer foundation because they've learned things as they've needed them rather than having it thrust on them.
>
> D: And that's a difficult thing for a teacher to do isn't it? To say 'look I know this looks slower, but I think, and I can't prove this, but I think

there are going to be firmer foundations for this person so that they will in the end write better.'

K: But we don't know that at the time, do we? We can only look backwards from children that we have taught.

The balance of interaction strategies

One of the approach's strengths is the encouragement for the teacher to become expert in knowing when to intervene and when to encourage and facilitate. Teachers do need to be aware of how they use these skills, and how these skills vary from child to child and the implications for whole class and group teaching. Gemma reflects on the necessary emphasis on individualized teaching.

G: I think it is not so much teaching in the formal sense of 'we are all doing this' or a whole group are doing this, it becomes far more individualized and as the need arises. I think you have to be a more resourceful teacher, because you have to have something ready just when that child needs it, or something up your sleeve, such as a book that could supplement a point to make it a bit more relevant.

Whole school policies

There is considerable pressure on schools to produce policies for the wide range of activities that take place during the year. The development of language throughout a school is enhanced when teachers are working in similar ways. Policies must be more than one sheet of A4 with a list of general statements. More work needs to be done to ensure that policies are living documents and that they give specific examples of what the school considers to be good practice. This good practice is identified and targeted where possible so that teachers know when they are working in similar ways. The role of the language coordinator in this cannot be over-emphasized. Karen felt that the set rules of traditional approaches to language were easier to establish as policy but that there were problems.

K: I think the more rules you have the less chance there is of them [the children] veering off on their own pathway and it does keep a tighter control. The problem then is that you also have a tight control over children's creativity and you can lose that. Creativity means the opportunity to think and react to your thoughts in your own individual way. If you have got traditional type rules then you haven't got the opportunities.

The balance between composition and transcription

This issue has dogged discussions about primary writing for many years, but it remains unresolved. At all levels in the school, from classroom to policy to communication with parents, this issue needs to be evaluated and action taken to ensure that an appropriate balance is achieved.

I have offered above eight significant points that suggest developments for the practice and theory of emergent literacy. These points are offered in the light of the work of schools and teachers who continue to achieve success with emergent writing in spite of the current hostility to anything that has a whiff of being 'progressive'. Teachers need a confident understanding of the theory of emergent writing, and high quality experience, in order to challenge the many simplistic views that will continue to be aired about the teaching of writing. One of Karen's comments in the interview summed up a sense of frustration with the regular attempts to link progressive practice with 'trendy teaching'.

K: Well we are looking at 'trendy teachers' who are coming up to 50 years old. You know I seem to have been a 'trendy teacher' for so long now. When do you ever stop, and should you ever stop?

THREE

The development of composition

When the process approach is used, specific compositional aspects of writing are given emphasis. The children are encouraged to make decisions on the nature of their planning, the audience, the content, the genre, the length, whether to collaborate or work alone, the amount of redrafting etc. Although the children are experiencing these compositional elements, the teacher needs to have clear ideas for extending the children's development. During writing workshop or emergent writing sessions the children will be at a variety of different stages in the writing process. The teacher needs to be able to interact effectively to move children forward when appropriate and to anticipate and extend compositional development. This teaching can be made easier if the teacher has clear frameworks in mind which categorize the important elements of written composition.

The distinction between composition and transcription has been addressed by a number of authors. Frank Smith (1982) provided a succinct description (Table 3.1).

Smith's diagram communicates this important distinction with simplicity and clarity. Composition refers to the author skills and the creative aspect of

Table 3.1

| Composition
(author) | Transcription
(secretary) |
| --- | --- |
| Getting ideas
Selecting words
Grammar | Physical effort of writing
Spelling
Capitalization
Punctuation
Paragraphs
Legibility |

Smith 1982: 20

the process. Transcription refers to the secretarial and presentational skills. It is necessary to recognize that the two sides are not mutually exclusive. For example, the task of selecting words appears as a compositional skill, but if a child rejects a word because they do not know how to spell it, this is partly a transcriptional issue. Similarly, in the transcription column the punctuation of sentences is closely tied to the child's semantic understanding of sentence structure, which can be seen as a compositional issue.

It has been recognized by many teachers that the two sides of this diagram often receive unequal treatment. As one teacher said, 'It's easier to plan punc- tuation and spelling lessons but teachers *are* interested in the content. We often share good pieces of writing in the staffroom.' Cato *et al.* (1992) found that an imbalance existed in their study that looked at approaches to initial literacy. In addition to questionnaires which 122 headteachers and 115 teachers completed, the research team visited 26 schools representing five LEAs for between half and one complete school day. One of the conclusions reached on the teaching of writing was as follows:

> In commenting on the teaching of writing, it is important to note what appeared to be a concentration on 'secretarial' aspects of written work: the focus in some cases on surface features of writing as opposed to matters relating to content, form, and style; the simplistic notions of 'redrafting' that prevailed in some classes; and the relative lack of exploi- tation of the word-processing facilities that were available to pupils in some cases, particularly with regard to redrafting.
>
> (Cato *et al.* 1992: 36)

This conclusion has been reached by many different people who have looked at the teaching of primary writing, including teachers, researchers, inspectors etc. Part of the reason for this unequal treatment lies in the difficulties that teachers face in conceptualizing, articulating and teaching composition. Tran- scription is often covered in much detail by breaking the area down into its constituent skills, but with composition this is not so straightforward. In spite of regular criticisms of this imbalance there are many teachers who continue to place undue emphasis on transcriptional aspects of writing.

Part of the problem for teachers comes in identifying the aspects of com- position that need to be taught. This is different from transcription, where the skills and concepts required seem to be easier to group and classify. In part this is historical, as in the past much attention has been devoted to tran- scription. Frameworks are needed that help teachers to conceptualize the skills and concepts related to compositional development.

In the course of this chapter I explore some of the complexities of compo- sition. In order to identify new ways of thinking about composition I examine the nature of teacher/pupil interaction during writing conference. By looking at my own and three other teachers' reflections I have created two frameworks that I hope will encourage people to think differently about composition. The frameworks are inevitably only starting points, but I hope that the contextual information will give other teachers the encouragement to continue searching for ways of thinking about the teaching of written composition.

The first framework was inspired by the reflections of three teachers who focused on their teaching of writing. (The reflections were part of a research project that looked at the teaching of writing – see Chapter 5.) In the course of the research a diagram emerged that illuminated the area of composition. The second framework resulted from the work of a school where I was Language Coordinator. This case study illustrates how the school established benchmarks for compositional development. The description of the process the school went through also illustrates how the classroom practice of the language coordinator fed into whole school development.

Three teachers' reflections on writing: helping children compose

The research focused on the teaching of writing. During the research the three teachers focused on one child and wrote their reflections and observations about the teaching of that child over the course of a year. Once a fortnight they filled in a data collection sheet that encouraged them to note what the child did, what the teacher did, and why, during a period of interaction. (The 'why' became an important aspect of the study, as it focused on the rationales and aims of the three teachers.) The teachers were interviewed once a fortnight to clarify the data and its early analysis. Here is an example from one of the data sheets where Keith reflected on a period of interaction.

Teacher (T):   Sat down next to Waqaas preparing to work with him.
Child (C):   Read me second draft of story using reading scheme characters. He explained also how he wanted to remove his final sentence (which closed the story), insert some more events, then re-use the same closing sentence.
T: 'So you're going to have this same bit at the end, but some more of the story first?' – checking that I had understood the intentions correctly.
C: 'Yes.'
T: 'Did you get this story from a book?' – checking if he is using more than just characters from a known source – encouraging him to reflect on his sources to aid his composition.
C: 'A bit. Some different things happen. In the book there's 3 children playing, in this it's 2 [pointing to a section of his writing]. I need a rubber.'
T: Showed him he could use a piece of paper stuck over the writing he wanted removed as it was quite lengthy – showing him a way to preserve appearance of quite a neat draft; showing an alternative way to alter composition.

This extract illustrates a range of compositional issues. The indication that this was a second draft shed light on Keith's practice of encouraging the children to work through a series of drafts and make decisions about the quality of their writing. Waqaas had chosen to write a story using characters from a reading scheme book. The drafting the child intended was fairly sophisticated. However, he might not have attempted it himself without Keith's help. Keith checked that the child was not relying too heavily on the original reading scheme text and encouraged the child to prove that his own text was significantly different.

By selecting reflections such as Keith's above, the analysis looked at how the teachers addressed composition in the course of their interaction. The analysis generated a framework that could be used by other teachers when thinking about their interaction or activity planning (Figure 3.1).

The complete diagram represents the compositional issues that teachers may want to address. It is divided into three sections which are represented by the three triangles; writers need teaching and support in these three areas. The 'ideas' triangle represents the writer's search for something to write about. The 'form' triangle represents the structural aspects of the piece of writing, including the genre. The 'language' triangle refers to the building blocks of writing, such as choice of words and putting the sentences together. Surrounding each triangle there are three keywords which further break down the concept and act as a prompt for planning, and to guide interaction. I describe each keyword, giving an example of its relevance to the classroom.

Ideas

- *Audience* – writing can lack focus and direction if the children do not have a particular audience in mind. Sometimes this may be the writer themselves. The natural audiences of the school community include peers, the class

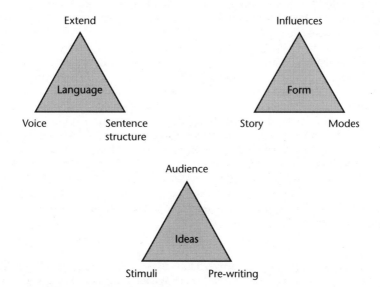

Figure 3.1 Composition framework

teacher, other adults in school, parents, relatives, family friends and children of different ages. Other audiences can be created, such as imaginary characters, local and national government figures, famous people etc. Another aspect of audience that needs thought is the idea that for many writers their specific audience is unknown and constantly changing; instead the writer has a general feeling for their audience's needs.

- *Stimuli* – the consideration for the teacher is whether to offer a stimulus or not. Sometimes a direct stimulus is appropriate in order to encourage writing. These stimuli take many forms, including stories, poetry, science experiments, drama, tape recording, artefacts, cross-curricular topics etc. Traditional approaches offers stimuli where topics are specified: the process approach offers stimuli that support the child's own decisions on topic. The specification of topic by the teacher alters the emphasis of compositional thinking from the global features such as title, audience and form, to decisions over the local features such as handling the genre, constructing sentences etc. Children should experience the thinking associated with both kinds of stimuli.
- *Pre-writing* – The teacher can offer various strategies to help the children before they start writing, such as brainstorm lists, planning frameworks, reflection on favourite texts, thinking about the range of texts available etc. Pre-writing is not meant in its old-fashioned sense; historically, pre-writing strategies were exercises the child had to do before it was felt they could write 'properly'.

Form

- *Influences* – Much of children's writing is inspired by other texts, television and film. An important part of developing composition is knowing how much one can use from other texts before it becomes 'copying'. The teacher encourages the child to reflect on how other texts influence their writing.
- *Story* – story holds an enduring fascination for children and as such, the genre needs particular attention. The children's understanding of story structure can benefit from direct intervention. At the start this might involve the appreciation of beginning, middle, main event, end. Once the awareness of structure is raised and discussed, children begin to generalize their own more complex ideas on story structure. These ideas can be extended further during writing conferences.
- *Modes* – children need to experience a range of modes of writing. (Britton (1970) called these 'forms' but Temple *et al.* (1982: 131) redefined them as modes.) The modes are less rigid than the analysis of individual genres. They allow for the developmental characteristics of children's writing where the different genres are often merged.

The 'expressive mode' is language that is close to the self, used to reveal the nature of the person, to verbalize his consciousness, and to exhibit his close relation to the reader. Expressive language is a free flow of ideas and feelings. Diary writing is a good example of this mode.

The 'transactional mode' is language concerned with getting things done. It involves giving information or instructions, and attempting to persuade and advise others. The instructions for a game that the children have invented or the steps taken to construct a model are examples of the transactional mode.

The 'poetic mode' uses language as a verbal construct, fashioned in a particular way to make a pattern. Language is used in the poetic mode as an art medium. Poetry is of course the prime example of this but stories also fit into this mode.

The notion of mode is particularly useful in the early years where the adult distinctions between the different genres are often blurred. However, these categories overlap at times. For example, children's narrative in the early years can often have an expressive quality about it as they use their personal experiences to structure the narrative. As children become more experienced they learn more about the characteristics of the various written genres which fit within these categories.

Language

- *Extend* – this refers to the necessity to constantly extend the range, complexity and richness of the language that children use. An example is the transition from ordinary narrative to that which offers lively and imaginative description. This necessity is also evident in writing that begs for questions from the reader to aid their complete understanding. An example of this is Adam's book called 'The Jungle' which illustrates the need for extended language.

  The gorilla is slicing a banana in half.
  The cheetah is hiding in the bushes; he ate a human being.
  He set the jungle on fire.
  The animals have run to the top of the hill, the fire is at the bottom of the hill.
  The tree is on fire, so are the coconuts and so is the floor.
  The fire put itself out.

- *Voice* – a difficult concept to teach. It refers to the style of the writer and their distinctive voice. Some children tend towards a terse, simple style while others can be extravagantly imaginative. The teacher's role is to first give ownership of the writing process to children. They can then be supported in the development of their own distinctive written voice.
- *Sentence structure* – the standard syntax of sentence structure could be regarded as a transcription skill. However, sentence structure has its own significance within the compositional process. The particular way that children structure sentences helps with the flow of the writing. Sentence structure is also influenced by genre, where for example the sentence structure of a science report will differ from that of a poem.

Using the framework: a classroom example

The framework can be used in two ways. The keywords provide a focus for interaction when helping the child's composition. It can also be used as a way of informing the planning of activities which have a focus on composition issues. The following example illustrates how I used the diagram as a planning prompt with my year five class. I wanted to address *influences*; however, the activity that the children took part in touched on several areas of the composition framework. The activity was also inspired by the work the children had done during writing workshop.

The class topic for the half term was 'water'. One of the children brought a newspaper article taken from a local paper (Figure 3.2). I wanted to use this as a way of building on the child's interest and to tackle a number of language skills/concepts with the class. The article had a flashback in the top right hand corner with the headline 'They think it's all over', referring to Yorkshire Water's view that the rain in November meant the drought was over. The headline in the subsequent article was 'It is now!'

The first part of the activity involved the children getting to grips with the article. Basically this was a series of comprehension questions:

Yorkshire Water

1 Read the article and write a summary of about 6 lines.
2 What does the bar chart tell you?
3 Look at the list of events in the middle of the page. What happened on November 15?
4 The headline at the top of the page has a double meaning. What are the two meanings?
5 What has made local residents happy?
6 You are going to design a newspaper article about water. Use the information books to decide the subject you are going to choose. Then write an article which uses as much of the information as possible. Early drafts on paper, final draft on newspaper style columns.

As you can see, part 6 is the section where the children were encouraged to handle a variety of texts and use information books as one of the influences for the information in their newspaper article. The first stage involved them skim reading and scanning to select a subject of interest to them. Once the subject had been chosen they had to decide which parts of the information they were to include in their article. At this stage I insisted that the new information should be assimilated and presented in their own language. This indicated their level of understanding of the new information. The story behind the article was to be imaginary, so this involved their story writing skills. However, the language of the story needed to be in the style of newspapers. In the past we had worked with the education officer of the local newspaper in various media activities, so we had available newsprint paper with ruled columns. For the final draft the children were able to cut and paste the various bits of text, headings, pictures, graphs etc. to fit within the newspaper style columns. Here are two examples from the children's work:

FLASHBACK . . . When heavy rainfall looked to have ended the drought in November

Yorkshire Water calls off threat of rota cuts and ends tankering

By CATHERINE O'CONNOR

THE threat of rota cuts has been lifted from thousands of Calderdale homes as reservoir levels in the district begin to rise.

Stocks for Calderdale and Kirklees now stand at 20.5 per cent, a figure which is still extremely low compared to normal January levels of well over 90 per cent.

Hundreds of residents whose lives were made a misery by the huge water tankering operation will breath a huge sigh of relief after Yorkshire Water also announced the end of efforts to replenish vital stocks by bringing water into West Yorkshire by road.

But the beleagured company, which announced last night it was withdrawing its application to the Department of the Environment for permission to impose rota cuts in Calderdale and Kirklees, is still being criticised for suspending emergency measures too soon.

The company did not resume full-scale tankering to the Albert treatment works, Pellon, Halifax, after the Christmas break, although emergency tankers were used when stocks fell to critical levels during the New Year thaw.

The operation to bring water to Kirklees from Selby will finish by the end of this week.

Emergency drought orders granted for the region's rivers and reservoirs will remain in force, as will the hosepipe ban and restrictions on use affecting much of Yorkshire.

Mr John Layfield, Yorkshire Water's director of production and technology, said: "Reservoir levels are now far higher than when we felt it necessary to apply for permission to impose rota cuts. Our application regarding rota cuts is therefore now no longer needed.

He believed the tankering operation had done the job of helping to stave off rota cuts.

"The rainfall we have had in the past week is equivalent to two months of tankering."

But Coun Stephen Pearson (Lib-Dem, Greetland/Stainland) said he believed the company was being short-sighted.

"I am concerned Yorkshire Water has stopped tankering just because we have had a blip in the weather. I am worried that when we get to August or September there will not be sufficient water in the reservoirs and we will be back to a hosepipe ban and the threat of rota cuts and tankering again."

Yorkshire Water spokeswoman, Tracy Wood, emphasised that the drought was not over and people still needed to save water.

"It is not viable to think we can fill the reservoirs using the tankering operation."

The infrastructure for emergency measures would be kept in place and the company would reinstate them if stocks fell again.

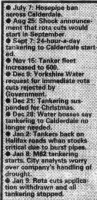

● July 7: Hosepipe ban across Calderdale.
● Aug 25: Shock announcement that rota cuts would start in September.
● Sept 7: 24-hour-a-day tankering to Calderdale started.
● Nov 15: Tanker fleet increased to 600.
● Dec 9: Yorkshire Water request for immediate rota cuts rejected by Government.
● Dec 21: Tankering suspended for Christmas.
● Dec 28: Water bosses say tankering to Calderdale no longer needed.
● Jan 2: Tankers back on Halifax roads when stocks critical due to burst pipes.
● Jan 8: M62 tankering starts. City analysts worry over company's handling of drought.
● Jan 9: Rota cuts application withdrawn and all tankering stopped.

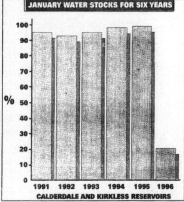

JANUARY WATER STOCKS FOR SIX YEARS

CALDERDALE AND KIRKLESS RESERVOIRS

WATER WATCH
Update

RESERVOIR STOCKS
YESTERDAY - 24.9 per cent
MONDAY - 23.4 per cent
FRIDAY - 21.2 per cent

RAINFALL AT WALSHAW DEAN
YESTERDAY - 8.7 mm
JAN TOTAL - 31.2 mm
JANUARY AVE - 133 mm

DEMAND (24 hours to 09.00hrs)
YESTERDAY - 59.8 thousand cubic metres. MONDAY - 60.5 thousand cubic metres

Figure 3.2

Tidal wave strikes terror into holiday makers

Yesterday a tidal wave hit Blackpool Tower, the tower fell into the Bloodhound Public House. 20 people were killed and 7 badly injured. Mr Oloworth the barman said, 'The crash was terrifying, the ceiling just fell down on everyone and bits of iron tumbled through the roof.'

Mr Oloworth is now in casualty. Doctors say his condition is serious but stable. Men were repainting the tower when the catastrophe occurred, unfortunately all the men died because of the gigantic drop of about 200 metres. Our reporter Jon Allen spoke to one of the men's wives. She said she had no idea what had happened until her next door neighbour came round and told her.

Tom caught the style of the newspaper language well. This did not surprise me, as he often showed his intelligent response to a range of issues during discussions. I felt, however, that he had relied mainly on his prior knowledge rather than explicitly including influences from other texts. He had read about tidal waves, but perhaps the writing does not show the new knowledge that he assimilated.

Rebecca was interested in animals:

Water pollution – get animals quick

The water has been polluted in the Pacific Ocean. A tanker has spilled all its oil and rescue boats are looking for animals. They have found lots of birds, fish, seals and many more.

The Blue Whale has been found with no oil on it but if it swims into the oil slick it will die. The manatee has been found with lots of oil in its fur. The rescue team has found about 30 of them. The oil workers are trying to get the oil out as fast as they can.

Rebecca used at least two books for the information which her news story was based on. At first she was going to use a freshwater animal that she had learned about, but I suggested she might need to consider sea creatures if the oil disaster was to be in the sea. The result of the conversation was her decision to use the manatee, which she thought would be more appropriate although there was still some uncertainty about its natural habitat.

As I reflected on the appropriateness of the activity I realized that it was only a starting point. The issue of influences had been covered mainly in an implicit way and I felt I needed other activities to raise the children's awareness. (A subsequent activity encouraged the children to examine how Jon Sciezka's story 'The True Story of the 3 Little Pigs' differed from the original.) Another issue was the text level of the original newspaper article; a significant minority of children needed much help in understanding some of the language, but the majority of children were able to tackle the task and extend their writing.

Each of the keywords in the diagram can act as the stimulus for an activity to develop compositional skills. In addition the framework can help to focus interaction with children.

Theory and research

It is clear to many teachers that learning to write is more difficult than learning to talk. The mental processes that help us learn to talk do have significant bearing on the learning of reading and writing, but each mode also has its own specific learning requirements. The links between the modes are perhaps rather more complex than was at first thought. Frank Smith's views that learning to read and write (which he called 'joining the literacy club') were very closely linked to learning how to talk, had significant implications for the way literacy was taught. Evidence from teachers and children would suggest that we need to examine these assumptions carefully. Why is it that some children are verbally expert but find reading and writing tasks difficult? Why do some proficient readers have difficulties with their writing?

Just as teachers sometimes neglect the area of written composition in the classroom, this has also been reflected in the amount of research. Beard (1984) commented that transcription had generally received more attention than composition in education studies and in teaching. Since that time, Bereiter and Scardamalia have spent many years examining written composition. They looked at the development of composition from the perspective of cognitive psychology.

Bereiter and Scardamalia (1987) outlined two possible models for composition. The first was the 'knowledge telling' model. They sum this model up in the words of a 12-year-old pupil.

> I have a whole bunch of ideas and write them down until my supply of ideas is exhausted. Then I might try to think of more ideas up to the point when you can't get any more ideas that are worth putting down on paper and then I would end it.
>
> (Bereiter and Scardamalia 1987: 159)

While children are writing they need various cues to sustain the knowledge telling model. The three cues are topic, discourse schema and text already produced. The topic of the writing may be teacher directed or the pupil's own choice. If, for example, the text was a piece of information about alligators for a display, the topic suggests certain elements that perhaps should be included, such as eating habits, hunting and use of the skin, dangers of alligators, habitat etc. Once the writing has been started the child also finds inspiration from the text that has already been written. By being encouraged to go back to the beginning and read through, it is hoped that the child will decide what needs to come next.

The genre and discourse schema of a piece of writing can help give the writer cues that sustain the writing. For example, when writing poetry, the notion of line and line length is quite different from the sentences of a story; indeed, line length is normally arbitrary in a story. The importance of line length is one element of poetry that children need to be aware of in order to support their writing. It is these general awarenesses that help the child structure their piece of writing within a flexible framework.

The imposition of detailed rules and complex genre categories is less helpful. If the approach to genre is too didactic and fixed, it fails to account for the many flexibilities that exist when authors write. For example, experienced writers play with the formal conventions to produce writing of originality. If you take The Jolly Postman by the Ahlbergs, the book is essentially a story about the postman's delivery round. However, it is also written in rhyming couplets.

Each house the postman visits has a different fairy tale character, and examples of different genres are available to be read, for example a letter, an invitation, a catalogue etc.

Bereiter and Scardamalia's 'knowledge transforming' model is more sophisticated than the knowledge telling one. The main difference is the process of textual change from first to last draft. Expert writers make a wide range of changes throughout the drafting process where the context and purpose necessitate this. This process develops their writing skills and enables them to transform their knowledge.

> The distinctive capabilities of the knowledge-transforming model lie in formulating and solving problems and doing so in ways that allow a two-way interaction between continuously developing knowledge and continuously developing text.
>
> (Bereiter and Scardamalia 1987: 162)

The knowledge transforming model is seen in children who have enthusiasm and commitment to their writing and who continue to develop a range of complex writing skills. Sometimes the evidence for this motivation is revealed in work they have done at home, where the changes may be made in collaboration with various members of the family and family friends.

Bereiter and Scardamalia offer five strategies for improving the teaching and learning of written composition, which I have slightly modified.

1 Children need to be taught that writing is not just about putting words on paper. The process crucially involves constant planning, and evaluation of that planning throughout the writing time. If the teacher exclusively sets titles for the children, planning and evaluation is limited.
2 The thinking that is necessary for composing needs to be modelled by the teacher. (Graves (1983) too is an advocate of teachers modelling the writing process.) This can take place during mini-lessons (see Chapter 1) using a flipchart.
3 The steps that are necessary in order to become a better writer should be clear in the minds of the children as well as the teacher. This is particularly true for composition; the subject needs to be discussed regularly. The possible complexities of the discussion will serve to develop the children's higher order thinking.
4 Children need to undertake writing that challenges them. Writing that the children feel confident with should be balanced with writing tasks that stretch the child's learning. The struggle to write the first piece of written argument is worthwhile even if the initial results are disappointing.
5 Structured routines and frameworks can help in the early stages of learning complex processes. However, the children need to be aware of the purposes for the frameworks. For example, a planning framework for stories can be useful but the children also need to understand why such planning can sometimes be counter-productive.

Sutcliffe (1991) transferred some of Bereiter and Scardamalia's ideas to a research project she did with teachers on an in-service BEd course. She found that the teachers all felt less confident and less aware of composition than of transcription. They were offered a series of activities to help them and the children improve their understanding of composition. Bereiter and Scardamalia called such activities 'consequential composing activities'; they are intended to develop the thinking strategies that lead to effective composition. An important element of these activities was the evaluation that the children had to do. Not only did they experience the activities, but they also had to evaluate the purpose and success of the activities. The teachers in the study found that the activities were useful in developing their own understanding of composition and the understanding of the children.

The activities used by Sutcliffe included the following: lists, where the children were encouraged to regularly make lists of words that would be useful in their writing; content generation was carried out in small groups where the children would discuss the kinds of information and content that were appropriate for a particular writing task; picture plans were used as a means of planning that helped children sequence events and were seen as a possible bridge between talking and writing; story stoppers were a reversal of the traditional story starters, and suggested that the children think about the end of a story in the hope that this would provide cues for the beginning and middle.

Parker (1993) looked at composition in terms of Topic, Audience and Form. He suggested that the topic is generally easier for the child where it is concrete, based on personal experience or based on something present at the time of writing. Topic is harder where it is abstract, new information, a past event, or of a technical/specialist nature. The one form that challenges this view is story. Story is often chosen by young children as their preferred form. Although children have direct personal experience of stories, the events they contain are often past events, are abstract, and regularly generate new information and ideas.

The notion that children should write for a range of audiences has been accepted for some time now. Although this is undoubtedly sensible, there is a potential difficulty with the assumption. Some audiences have greater importance for children than others. An audience contrived by the teacher for the purpose of an activity may be less significant to the child than their peer group, who discuss, praise, occasionally ridicule and generally take interest in the writing when it is published and shared. This issue has implications for the children's motivation to write. The 1988 APU survey of language performance revealed that 'not less than two out of ten pupils have developed negative views about writing by the time they are eleven' (Gorman et al. 1989: 57). Children's motivation is enhanced when they decide on the most appropriate audience. The process approach has had remarkable success in generating increased motivation both for teachers to teach writing and for children to learn. By combining the process approach with set writing tasks, a balance can be achieved between the controlled development of necessary understandings, and maintaining the motivation to write.

A whole school approach to composition

The flexibility of the process approach can be a benefit for the teacher's professional development in addition to the positive learning experiences for the children. The approach fosters a search for fundamental questions about the teaching and learning of writing. The following example of school practice shows how the language coordinator carried out some action research in order to clarify the area of composition.

During writing workshop the children in the class were helped to organize their writing by using a writing folder. A label was stuck on the outside of the folder (see Chapters 1 and 6) to enable the teacher to monitor progress in composition and transcription. It was felt that the written observation of children's behaviour while writing would offer clues as to how to teach them better. In addition the observations might offer insights about the process of writing. As often as possible, notes were made about the nature of the interaction with the child during writing workshop or in the writing area of the classroom. An example of these kinds of observation is given in Chapter 6.

The language coordinator spent two years with the same class. The labels on the children's folders were a record of two years' interaction with the children. By analysing this data it was possible to search for the answers to a number of questions. One of these questions was, 'How can I map out the area of written composition?' This question was also being asked by other teachers in the school.

The observations on the writing folders needed reducing to a manageable format. The teacher's observations and reflections were coded and classified to identify key areas. Figure 3.3 illustrates the five key areas that emerged in relation to the teaching and learning of composition.

1 *Convey meaning*: initially all writers need a reason to do this.
2 *Organize time and resources*: they need a time and a place to write. The resources should facilitate the widest possible range of writing.
3 *Generate ideas*: during writing workshop the children are encouraged to generate their own ideas for writing.
4 *Text structure*: the organization of the words on the page.
5 *Reader–writer connection*: consideration of the reader's potential needs and interests. Consideration of style and audience etc.

Figure 3.3 simultaneously illustrates both developmental characteristics of composition and the process of writing. For each key word the statements above and below reflect possible stages of development in the direction of the arrows. These were compiled by taking the most common classroom observations made on the writing folder labels. The process of writing is reflected by a starting point at the left of the diagram moving to the right. This linear picture of the writing process is in contrast with the recursive strategies of most writers that are indicated by the cyclic nature of the longer line.

Looking above the 'convey meaning' box, the first observation is 'nature of meaning behind pictures'. This statement reflected the way that some children described in detail the significance of their picture whereas others simply named the objects and had to be encouraged to offer more information. At this point the teacher was able to scribe for the child in order to show them how their description looked in writing. One of the observations underneath the 'convey meaning' box says 'message can be read by reader without help

Convey meaning

- Intertextuality. Referring to other texts within child's own text, e.g. traditional stories.
- Metalinguistic awareness, i.e. ability to reflect on own language in an abstract way, e.g. playing with messages; codes; jokes etc.
- Mixing numbers and letters; extent and level of understanding.
- Ability to remember meaning over time. Percent accuracy when rereading text.
- Use of labelling strategy for objects or interest in children's names.
- Nature of meaning behind pictures.

- Writing carries a message. Where is the child's development in this?
- Can the child express written meaning in more than one language?
- Amount of text related to amount of meaning.
- Understands difference between copying and writing.
- Message can be read by reader without help from writer.
- Uses standard English effectively.

Organize time and resources

- Drafting skills.
- Controlling texts in progress. Use of writing folder/book.
- Pre-writing strategies. Delaying tactics. Ability to overcome blocks.
- Amount of support needed from teacher/adult.
- Nature and amount of collaboration.

- Motivation and independence to do these.
- Choice of resources. Types of paper, pencils etc.
- Decisions on number of pages in little book.
- Continuing writing over a period of days or finishing quickly.
- Regularity of writing and length of time spent writing.

Generate ideas

- Videos, true stories, exploring adult forms, e.g. poem, information, text.
- Understanding variety of sources for ideas, e.g. other children, books, old writing.
- Ability to take risks, e.g. invent spellings.

- Ease at generating ideas.
- Increasing complexity of vocabulary; word selection.
- Developing a range of forms or preferring to practise one form predominantly, e.g. story.
- Ability to use less common forms such as argument.

Text structure

- Where is the child in the gradual process away from personal narrative towards more abstract writing?
- Understanding of start, middle and end and other genre-related issues.
- Length of text and reasons for choosing a particular length.

- Concept of text, sentence, word, space, letter.
- Unity of text and relationship to title.
- Use of cause and effect.
- Clause structure and nature of link words.

Reader–writer connection

- Surprising or deliberately familiar use of language for artistic effect.
- Developing a style as a writer.
- Ability to understand and use publishing cycle in the classroom.
- Influence of family, particularly older brothers and sisters.

- Wants to take text home.
- Relationship with teacher as 'important' reader.
- Clarity and necessary explicitness.
- Willingness to enter dialogue about writing with other readers.
- Ability to express strong emotions or to write in a detached way.

Figure 3.3

from writer'. This observation is developmentally further down the line and is reflected by its position in relation to the key word in the box.

The use of the process approach enabled the teacher to observe a range of writing and literate behaviours that illuminated the area of composition. By collecting and analysing these observations, a framework emerged that helped to structure both interaction and future activity planning. The model also served to support other teachers in the school. To conclude the chapter I briefly describe the way the framework contributed to whole school understanding.

Following a period of whole school development on language and literacy the teachers were keen to look at possible benchmarks for children who had experienced emergent writing and writing workshop. The language coordinator organized meetings with year group teams to discuss their expectations for children at various stages throughout the school. Most teams found the composition benchmarks more difficult to articulate and agree than the transcription benchmarks. The action research that the language coordinator had done with his class, and the resulting framework, helped him offer support to his colleagues as they agreed the benchmarks.

If we take the composition side of Table 3.2, number 3 shows what the teachers expected from most children at the end of year two (the confusing numbering is a result of the subsequent move towards National Curriculum years). 'Occasionally will write several pages of text' implied that the child had a good level of motivation and, given the space and time, would write at length; often this would be a story. Appropriate text length was an important aspect of compositional understanding. 'Understands difference between what is learned by copying as opposed to writing': this statement reflected the necessity for children and teachers to understand the distinction. It was felt that writing by copying helped mainly with the presentational aspects of writing; it did little to support composition. Both children and teachers needed to reflect on this issue.

The benchmarks that the school created helped the teachers plan for and monitor the development of writing. By making the distinction between composition and transcription explicit, the school was beginning to address the issue of balance between these two important elements of the writing curriculum.

I have presented two possible frameworks that conceptualize the area of written composition. The first was created from three teachers' reflections on their own teaching of writing. The second was generated by closely observing children who were writing, and recording those observations. Both offer something distinctive but they also have overlaps – not surprisingly, as the focus was the teaching and learning of writing. The use of such frameworks can enable teachers and schools to ensure an appropriate focus on composition.

Table 3.2 School benchmarks

Composition		Transcription
Confident to make marks independently. Knows difference between pictures and writing/ numbers. Can tell you about pictures. Understands that writing has a message.	0	Selects and uses writing resources appropriately. Controls a variety of mark making resources. Beginning to understand notions of text.
Understands what a text is. Can use own ideas to write and convey them to an adult. Growing understanding of stories and their structure. Pictures are in greater detail, with explanations becoming more complex.	1	Understands difference between skills work and other writing. Recognizes and can write letters of the alphabet. Aware that there is a link between sounds and symbols, particularly consonants.
Confident to write independently or when directed. Exploring greater range of writing. Can remember meaning of text the next day. May have temporary lack of confidence due to new understandings of transcription skills.	2	Makes sensible decisions about use of materials. Knows all the letters of the alphabet by name and can relate to sounds. Pencil control confident. Understands names of large text structures (e.g. story, poem, information text). Beginning to understand smaller structures (e.g. word, space, letter).
Writing can be read by adult without help from child. Occasionally will write several pages of text. Understands difference between what is learned by copying as opposed to writing. Developing increasing range of directed and undirected forms. Publishing cycle developing.	3	Phonetic spelling. Concept of word and space established. Initial letter usually standard. Knows some standard spellings. Some cursive letter shapes developing.
Aware of reading needs, e.g. and, then. Organizes writing folder and work books effectively. Confident to try a variety of forms, including information texts.	4	Transitional spelling stage. Beginning to reflect on visual nature of English spelling. Knows when capitals are used. Beginning to use capitals and full stops.
Can read through own work and make a variety of changes, not just spelling. Can use computer as a drafting tool. Publish book effectively from initial idea to product.	5	Mainly standard spelling and letter formation. When required can present work attractively. Understands full stop and sentence structure. May use other punctuation marks. Developing upper and lower case.
Uses information sources and writing to learn. Sets up own projects. Reflects on own language use, e.g. messages, codes, jokes etc. Confident with story, poem, information text, argument. Aware of reader's needs. Personal style.	6	Standard spelling, mistakes self-corrected with dictionary or spell-check. Cursive writing. Standard punctuation including commas. Presents writing appropriately depending on audience. Calligraphy, lettering styles. Developing keyboard skills. Vocabulary and sentence complexity increasing.

FOUR

Transcription

One of the important tasks the teacher faces is to ensure a balance between composition and transcription. In the last chapter I suggested that the process approach supports a natural emphasis on composition. As with any approach to writing, transcription also requires much teacher support. In this chapter I look at ways in which teachers can support transcription within and alongside the process approach.

Although all the transcription skills and concepts are important, spelling often receives a higher priority than the others. I believe that this reflects the fact that many teachers regard the learning of standard spelling as one of the most significant elements of transcription, if not the most significant. For this reason I have decided to devote the main part of this chapter to spelling, but prior to this I take a brief look at handwriting and punctuation. The chapter goes on to offer strategies for the teaching of spelling when using the process approach. Examples of children's writing are related to the five stages of development; these stages are also examined in relation to the interaction strategies of the teacher. The chapter concludes with a look at some of the theory and research in the area.

Handwriting and punctuation

The development of flowing and legible handwriting is something that lends itself well to decontextualized exercises. It is difficult to focus properly on handwriting during writing workshop because there are so many other issues that take priority. Drafting for publication purposes is one occasion when presentation issues are addressed, and this may include looking at the legibility of the handwriting; but I believe that the development of good handwriting needs weekly guided practice for many children. This is particularly important when you consider the research evidence that suggests that good handwriting often supports the development of spelling.

'Good' handwriting implies handwriting that allows the writer to write flu-
ently and that is clearly legible for the reader. If this is the case, some children
will achieve this earlier than others. It is pointless for the children who achieve
good handwriting early to do the same exercises as those children who need
more practice. One possible solution to this is to have a range of tasks available; this enables those children who do not need further practice to select
different tasks. These tasks might be different altogether or could involve more
advanced handwriting techniques such as calligraphy and italic writing. The
implication behind this is that whole class teaching of handwriting, particularly at the latter end of Key Stage 2, is often inappropriate.

The teaching of handwriting usually involves children copying from a
sequential series of copy sheets. Although for many areas of the language curriculum this would be inappropriate, for handwriting the practice of appropriate pen movements is well served by some published resources. Christopher
Jarman (1979) offered a well thought out handwriting scheme that included
background information on the history of handwriting instruction and
developmental profiles of children's writing at different stages. He identified
eight basic patterns that are the foundations of a 'basic modern hand'. He also
recommended that the teacher should demonstrate on a board how various
patterns and letters are formed, and that children should be given support and
guidance during handwriting practice. However, he has been criticized for
being too prescriptive in relation to the angles and specific letter shapes that
he recommends. Rosemary Sassoon's (1990) work is less prescriptive but, like
Jarman, she recommends whole school policies and regular weekly practice
throughout the primary school.

Hall and Robinson (1996) suggested that punctuation has been very much
neglected in the literature that looks at children's writing development. I
recognize that, to a certain extent, I am about to perpetuate that neglect.
However, for those readers who are particularly interested in this subject, Hall
and Robinson do give a thorough review of punctuation.

Children commonly acquire knowledge of punctuation in broad stages.
Usually the first concept to be established is that of the sentence. The full stop
is developed first, followed by special marks such as question marks and exclamation marks. Within this developmental sequence individual children may
occasionally experiment with the different marks, sometimes resulting in, for
example, a rash of exclamation marks throughout a piece of writing. Commas,
speech marks, colons, semicolons etc. usually follow later.

The concept of the sentence can be a difficult one for the teacher to teach
and the pupil to learn. Often it can be confused by the mistaken idea that we
speak in sentences. Speech is quite different from writing in this respect.
Speech is delivered in information units and is separated by pauses to breathe,
ums and ahs, and interjections by the other speaker. It is fragmented and is
structured differently from writing. Writing is structured in sentences and
clauses; it allows the writer to reflect and redraft the message, unlike speech,
which is spontaneous. Even defining the sentence can be difficult. The best
approach is for the teacher to help the child understand the nature of this
complexity and encourage them to work out the general characteristics of sentences through the experience of writing. Sometimes, suggesting the idea that

a sentence usually focuses on one main idea can help. The children can prove or disprove such statements through their writing experience, supported by the teacher's interaction.

In the early stages children often substitute the full stop by 'and' or 'then'. It can be useful for the teacher to recommend that the child looks carefully at the use of 'and' or 'then' and decides whether a full stop would be better. For this to happen and for more general punctuation errors to be corrected, the child needs to understand the necessity to proofread writing themselves or with the help of a partner. Often, missing full stops represent the child's attention to composition in an early draft. It is not that they do not understand where the full stops should be placed, but it is more to do with the punctuation not being an automatic skill. This difficulty is linked to the child's developing ability to proofread.

Handwriting and punctuation seem to attract less controversy than spelling. Teachers often feel confident to develop these skills within a variety of approaches to the teaching of writing. The development of spelling is an issue that often dominates teachers' concerns, interaction and activity planning. Within the structure of the process approach the teacher must feel confident to evaluate and support spelling development at recognizable stages.

Spelling

The first priority for developing spelling during writing workshop is to establish 'invented spelling'. Invented spelling involves the children 'having a go' at the spellings based on their current knowledge of words. This enables them to continue writing without having to continually stop and ask for words or substitute simpler words because they do not know how to spell a particular word. Some children find this idea difficult at first if they are used to an emphasis on correct spelling at all times. Sometimes an unrealistic attitude to correctness has been taught at home, or by previous teachers if the school does not have a well established language policy. Although the final goal for all teachers is standard spelling, they recognize that children need a classroom and home ethos that encourages and recognizes development. Therefore a balance must be found in terms of the appropriate focus on correctness in relation to the child's development.

When children invent their spellings the teacher gets a realistic picture of their spelling development and is able to decide on the strategies and activities that will be needed to support spelling for individual children and for the class as a whole. Invented spelling does not preclude the use of a range of strategies that give the child the words that he/she needs. It is a starting point for development and enables the teacher to manage writing workshop. It benefits the children because they are encouraged to pose and solve their own spelling problems, and to develop the important generalizations that enable them to become standard spellers.

For many children the experience of writing workshop, set writing and spelling tasks, the teacher's support during writing conference and their own developing proofreading skills, will be enough to enable them to learn standard spelling. However, there may be some children who require differ-ent support strategies. The use of word books and word cards is common prac-tice. These can be particularly helpful for some children to develop their knowledge of the alphabet and as a resource for common words. Many of the most common English words are phonetically irregular, and the use of word cards can support the visual whole word learning strategies. In a small number of cases the teacher must guard against an over-reliance on the word card; some children continually stop and search for each word of their text. This has the effect of bringing the composition almost to a standstill. It restricts their learning because of the minimal amount of writing that goes on the page, resulting in a restricted focus for interaction during writing conference.

For older children the use of a dictionary can be helpful. The classic dilemma with dictionaries is the fact that in order to use one effectively you need to have a good idea of the first few letters of the word anyway. The other problem is that many dictionaries designed for children simply do not have the words that they want to look up. For younger children the dictionaries that contain a restricted selection of commonly used words are useful. Pictures often enhance these, but the problem is that many words that are not nouns simply do not have a relevant connected picture. For older children it is perhaps better to have standard high quality adult dictionaries, partly because the words that motivate them to search tend to be ones that are rarely included in dictionaries for children.

Word lists displayed in the classroom are a common idea. Sometimes these are topic related or specifically related to the language needed for an activity. During writing workshop it can be useful to start a list of words that children are commonly misspelling. They can write the standard versions on the list themselves. This has the added bonus of giving the teacher an indication of commonly misspelled words. These can then be fed into other activities and games that take place during the week.

During writing conference the support for spelling that the teacher gives the child is vital. Having prioritized issues for development based on the balance between composition, transcription, the child's development and the context, the teacher often feels the need to talk about spelling. There will be occasions when the teacher decides to check all the child's spellings. Often this will happen after the child has done their own proofreading and prior to publi-cation. However, it is usually counter-productive to correct all the child's spelling errors. This can be a rather negative experience that does little to help the child's spelling development. It is far better for the child and/or the teacher to select between one and three spelling errors and focus on these in more depth.

The following extract indicates how a writing conference that was focused on spelling might proceed:

T: Can you see a word that you have spelled wrong?
C: Yes, 'could'.
T: You've got the 'c', the 'u' and the 'd' right. Do you know any of the letters that are missing?
C: No.

T: It looks like this. [Writes 'could' on a piece of scrap paper.] Which letters did you miss?

C: 'O' and 'L'.

T: Do you know any other words that are spelled like 'could'?

C: Yes, 'should'.

T: Well done. What about 'count'?

C: That's not the same.

T: It doesn't sound the same, but the first three letters are the same aren't they?

C: Mmm.

T: How will you remember the word next time?

C: Well I know that cold is c-o-l-d so I could remember to put a 'u' in the middle of cold.

T: I could get a cold!

C: Yes.

T: Will you do 'Look, Cover, Write, Check' on 'could' and these other two words?

It is not always possible or desirable to discuss spelling in this detail, but this kind of interaction during writing conference is regularly necessary. The teacher applied a number of strategies in the extract. The child had been encouraged to proofread his work before the teacher would comment. In this instance the teacher wanted to give positive feedback on the letters that the child had spelled correctly to support his self-esteem. She then encouraged the child to locate one of the words he had spelled wrong. The teacher did not want to correct all the child's spellings because there were too many, and she felt that in this context it would have been counter-productive. She focuses on one word in depth so that the child will learn some strategies that will support the learning of other words.

The teacher encouraged the child to look at the visual similarities between 'could' and 'count'. For many children at the transitional spelling stage, the ability to recognize the limitations of their phonic strategies is important. More and more they need to be able to see the visual similarities between words. This is connected to their understanding that many words that sound the same have different meanings, for example 'their' and 'there'.

An individualized spelling task

The strategies that the teacher used in the example above, and others that emerge in the course of writing workshop, can inform the planning for set activities. The following grid represents a spelling activity that I used regularly with my Year 5 class. By reflecting on my interaction during writing conference I became aware of various skills and concepts that I felt the children needed to address.

The words that are already part of the table were examples for the children if they were unclear how to approach the task. For the first column the children had to look back through various pieces of writing and identify words

Table 4.1 Individualized spelling activity

Word	Breakdown	Difficult part	Similar words 1	2	3	4
1 there	t + here	er	their	the	here	then
2 heard	h + ear + d	ea	heart	hear	earn	earned
3 tomorrow	to + morrow	orrow	tomato	morning	borrow	follow
4						
5						

that they had spelled wrong and continued to have difficulties with. The children whose spelling was standard were encouraged to locate words from a dictionary that they felt could be useful to them in the future. This element of choice within a structured framework enabled the children to choose words that were of particular relevance to them. We all have different problem spellings, and activities need to reflect this reality.

The second column involved the children in breaking the word into relevant visual letter patterns. This idea came from my reflections on the children's general spelling difficulties at the particular age. It was also informed by the work of Cripps and Peters (1990) and the notion that knowledge of morphemes is an important aid to becoming a standard speller (a morpheme is the smallest meaningful part of a word). I used the idea of morpheme flexibly and found that the 106 two-letter words in the English language were an interesting aspect of this. By interacting with the children it became evident that some found this difficult. I helped them to group the letters in more appropriate patterns if they struggled with this.

'Difficult part' was designed to take account of the way that we not only struggle with different words but that, within those words, we have particular letters or letter strings that we find difficult. Often the key to learning a spelling lies in identifying problem letters and devising a strategy that will enable you to remember the word next time. The children had to identify the letter or letters that they found difficult to remember.

The final part of the task encouraged the children to find four words that were similar to each word that they had chosen. My examples again indicated that I wanted them particularly to concentrate on visual similarities. Those children at an earlier stage of development tended to find phonetic similarities, and this in part reflected the teaching they had encountered in the past that had emphasized phonic strategies. Although phonic teaching is important, there comes a point when it is vital that the children begin to recognize the limitations of phonics and the importance of visual spelling strategies.

The spelling task that I have described was in part inspired by the work during writing workshop. It became clear that the children had a range of needs but that a substantial number shared common problems. The activities that I devised needed to reflect that reality.

When invented spelling is adopted as a strategy there are sometimes concerns that this does not provide enough structure. The teacher may feel that it is more difficult to structure the child's spelling development. The first part of the answer to this problem lies in the careful observation of children's spelling development within the invented spelling regime. The second part of the answer involves the teacher using the evidence of development as a way of tailoring their interaction and activities to emphasize the strategies that are of most relevance to the child. If we look at invented spelling development, what general stages can be identified?

The development of invented spelling

Children who are encouraged to use invented spelling usually pass through a series of recognizable stages. In the past, the over-use of 'copywriting' and the

Table 4.2   Spelling – developmental stages

Mark making and letter strings
This category covers the child's earliest attempts at mark making in nursery and reception through to letter string sequences which are often influenced by particularly familiar letters (e.g. in the child's name) and what appears to be almost random choice.

Initial letter
Here the child is becoming aware that a limited form of sound–symbol correspondence exists. They may use consonants more confidently than vowels. Much work has been done to establish the concept of word and space. The child knows the names of the letters and is aware that those letters can be linked to a variety of sounds.

Phonetic
Invented spelling is now characterized by over-generalization of phonic strategies. The child needs to become aware of the limitations of phonics and be shown the visual nature of the English spelling system. Whole words need to be learned from memory in the context of the piece the child is writing or reading.

Transitional
Standard spellings are occasionally being used; invented spelling is characterized by fewer phonetic strategies and more visual strategies. The number of letters in a word is often standard and several of them will be correct.

Standard
The majority of words are spelled in a standard way. In the middle of a series of drafts the child may decide to use a dictionary or computer spell check. More and more the child will be able to rely on visual strategies to predict spellings of an ever-increasing vocabulary.

use of a restricted vocabulary of standard spellings meant that the teacher had less opportunity to see and reflect upon spelling development. The following section outlines the stages of development (Table 4.2) and gives examples of children's writing produced during writing workshop to illustrate them. It is important to bear in mind that the use of developmental stages presents a convenient picture; true development is rarely so straightforward. However, the stages can help to reassure teachers and parents that the children are developing in a predictable way.

Mark making and letter strings
Zara was at an early stage of development. She was bilingual, speaking Punjabi and English. The teacher was impressed by her creativity and motivation but was carefully monitoring her development. She had been working in the role-play area that had been organized as an office. While sitting at the typewriter she produced these strings of letters and numbers (Figure 4.1). The teacher wanted her to assign meaning to the marks, but Zara said, 'I write 765443211, just letters. I want to be a teacher.' The text had been folded and placed into an envelope that she had made. For Zara, the construction and modification of forms for her writing was an important part of the process. For example,

765443211

9op07uy6t5 4e3w2q1ghytfreeswaqzxvbhhmooiiiiuuystre-pooooooi

543223321344567890-=poiuuytrwqasddfghhjk

213467890

fghtrewqtyuiogpiasdff

h

jk

jhn f777 99oi

7uy6t5r4e32qw r yghujlky578

eyhnnbvvfftgfreee e

6 444 443 3

uuytt666 666

Figure 4.1

on another occasion what started as a Christmas card was cut up to become
a game where 'first you fold this like this . . . two each'.
   Darren produced the piece of writing in the writing area (Figure 4.2).
The letters are carefully formed and the handwriting moved from left to right.
The teacher scribed the standard English equivalent underneath to emphasize
the importance of meaning and so that they could compare the difference. The

A boy was chucking stones
at me and then I told

Miss and he had to stand

by the wall and then he

came off the wall and

threw some stones at me.

Figure 4.2

teacher encouraged the child to focus on the concept of words and word spaces by asking him to point carefully at each word as he read the standard form.

Initial letter

Ishtaq produced this book in the writing area of the classroom (Figure 4.3). He had been directed to work there, and the stapled booklet was one of the resources that had been prepared for the children. The teacher wrote underneath because the book was to be kept as a record of the child's development and she wanted to be sure she could remember the meaning. The teacher was interested in the way that Ishtaq used the old fashioned 'papa' and 'mama' throughout. Like many of the children, this child treated each page as a separate incident. This made the full text rather disjointed. However, each page consists of two speakers who each say one phrase. The last page alters this structure and this adds to the shock of the ending. The text is also linked and given some unity by the references to mama and papa. The full text was as follows:

'Papa, what are you saying?'
'I am saying that I like my mum.'
'What has happened to my shoes?'

WOT HAZ
HPD TO
MAY SOW Z
I DOT NO

PAP WT
RYYOSAVAKG AYMM
SAYEG TAT
ILAK MIY
MUM

"What has happened to my shoes?"
"I don't know."

Papa what are you saying? I am saying
that I like my mum

Figure 4.3

to my mum and Dad

One day to romens
was going to a
hather Land and the
to romens got
Cart in a tarat and
the PiePoL was the
hoJibs and the
romens was very Sade
and one of the romens
had a arrow went
in his haed the
romen was buring the
Other romen.

Figure 4.4

'I don't know.'
'The church is blowed up.'
'Why is the church blowed up?'
'Mama, what is that boy doing?'
'That boy is stupid, he is jumping on the train.'
'Mama! Papa has died.'

Phonetic
Neil produced his story 'The big fight with the Romans and the Hojibs' during regular writing workshop sessions (Figure 4.4). The teacher liked the way he had used an historical feature to give him the idea for a story and had added his own ingredients. Neil had started the year not really enjoying writing, and this book marked an important change in his motivation. He wrote pages and pages of text, and sometimes his enthusiasm resulted in unnecessary repetition. The teacher decided to praise Neil for his improved motivation and to check future texts for too much repetition.

Transitional
David is at the transitional spelling stage. He excelled at mathematics but found writing rather difficult. Even though he enjoyed writing workshop more than set tasks, he still found the writing difficult. His main difficulty was

In less than ten seckond

Chapter 3 the hide a way

They got took back to the mans scret. Hide out where there
wos five outher people who look ranthd nasty people. They put
chris and sophey in a cage and lockked the done. They wall away to there
Table a few meters away from the cage they sat down and sturter to
think. Then Shophey had a plan they notest a Handel in the cage so they
piled the Handel a arrrrrrrrrrrrrrrrrrrrrrrrrrrr
rr Ed!

They landed in a bed of money
"money" cried chris
"____" said Sophy
Are you Shrve it is said Chris   ?
"I am Shrve I am sure" Said sophey
"Whats that over there" said Chris
It wos a hote in the wall
"Shad we shouldt we. yes We will" Chris said
"OK" sophy Said
So they went thag the Hore Hole and looked around. There wo severds
dooes. Sophey went through the first and chris went thorvu the
seventh hore. They both met up. So this time they went
Togthr and came to two hores this time this time they split up
there got sperteat Sophey wos under a table with
The same people who was put them in the cage and then
Sophy shove chris in the cage the people wes slees
ing sleping drugs in his mouth ....

If you whont to find out what happn
reed the neto ishove

Figure 4.5

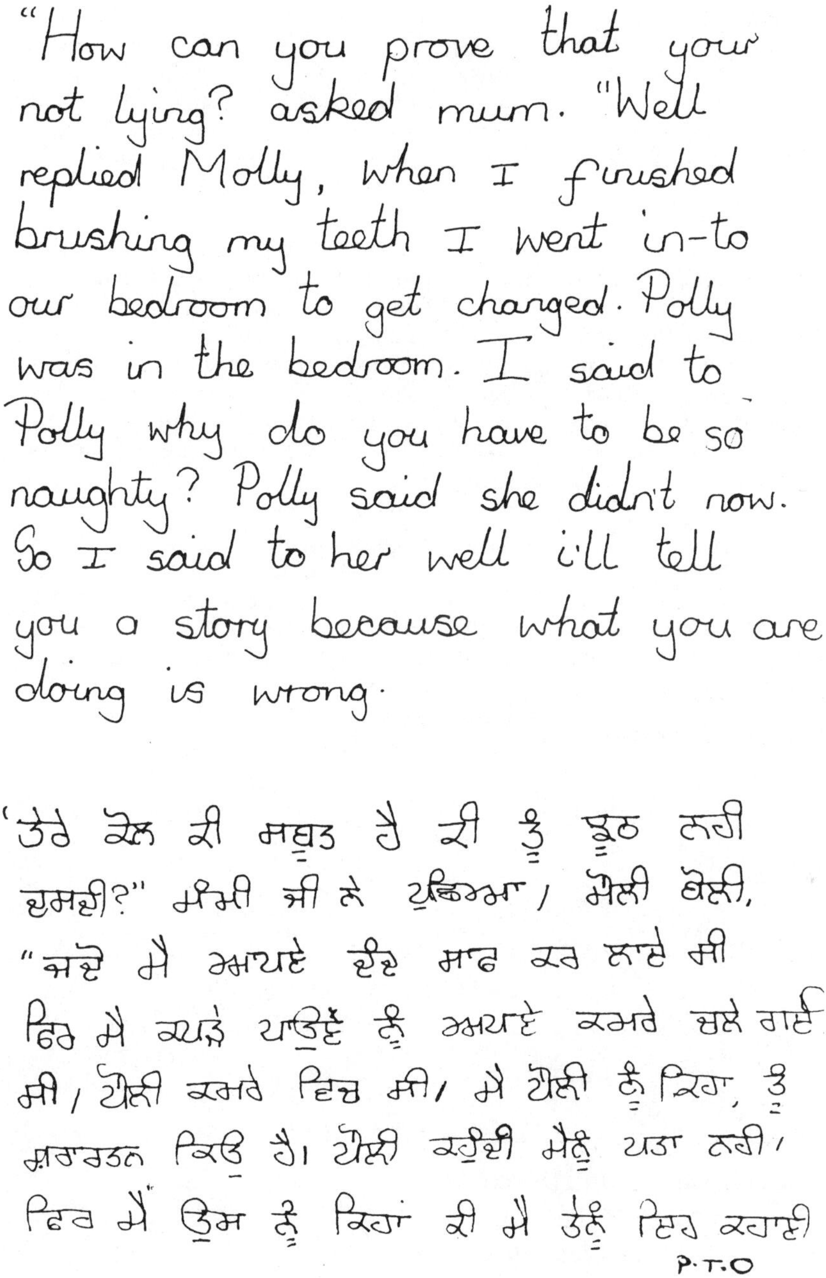

"How can you prove that your
not lying? asked mum. "Well
replied Molly, when I finished
brushing my teeth I went in-to
our bedroom to get changed. Polly
was in the bedroom. I said to
Polly why do you have to be so
naughty? Polly said she didn't now.
So I said to her well i'll tell
you a story because what you are
doing is wrong.

'ਤੇਰੇ ਕੋਲ ਕੀ ਸਬੂਤ ਹੈ ਕੀ ਤੂ ਝੂਠ ਨਹੀ
ਬੁਲਦੀ?" ਮੰਮੀ ਜੀ ਨੇ ਪੁੱਛਿਆ, ਮੌਲੀ ਬੋਲੀ,
"ਜਦੋ ਮੈ ਆਪਣੇ ਦੰਦ ਸਾਫ ਕਰ ਹਾਟੇ ਸੀ
ਫਿਰ ਮੈ ਕਪੜੇ ਪਾਉਣੂ ਨੂੰ ਆਪਣੇ ਕਮਰੇ ਚਲੇ ਗਈ
ਸੀ, ਪੌਲੀ ਕਮਰੇ ਵਿਚ ਸੀ, ਮੈ ਪੌਲੀ ਨੂੰ ਕਿਹਾ, ਤੂ
ਸ਼ਰਾਰਤਨ ਕਿਉ ਹੈ। ਪੌਲੀ ਕਹੀਂਦੀ ਮੈਨੂੰ ਪਤਾ ਨਹੀ,
ਫਿਰ ਮੈ ਉਸ ਨੂੰ ਕਿਹਾਂ ਕੀ ਮੈ ਤੈਨੂੰ ਇਕ ਕਹਾਣੀ
P.T.O

Figure 4.6

selecting suitable ideas and the subsequent slow speed of his first draft. David spells many words using standard spelling (Figure 4.5). He is using visual patterns but sometimes he selects the wrong pattern, for example 'outher' instead of 'other'; 'dore' instead of 'door'; 'notest' instead of 'noticed'. The teacher encouraged him to think of methods for remembering the correct patterns, and to commit the words to memory using 'look, cover, write, check'.

Standard

Sunita started 'The Naughty Twin' during a writing workshop session (Figure 4.6). Her teacher suggested that she might like to try a dual language text. Having completed the first draft in English, she took it home and asked her mother to help her with the written Punjabi. The teacher was interested in the idea that the child's naughtiness could be dealt with by a story. She wondered whether this came from the morals implicit in traditional stories. As well as a number of minor errors Sunita substitutes 'now' for 'know'. This is a common problem for more experienced spellers. The word that was used is spelled correctly but it is the wrong word for the context. The teacher helped the child to link the appropriate meaning with the correct spelling.

Bernadette's poems were written in response to a writing competition held during a school literacy week (Figure 4.7). The children were given the opportunity to take part in writing workshop at any time during the week unless other special events were taking place. Bernadette had benefited from weekly poetry reading sessions where the children chose poetry to read and performed it for the children in the class. The teacher knew that some of the poems in the selection had been influenced by professional poetry, but Bernadette had added much imagination of her own.

My Cats

My cats are very funny
very very funny.
But once I watched the telly
The cars went round the corner
My cat ran round the telly
To see where they had gone.

Figure 4.7

Each of the spelling stages requires teacher interaction that supports the particular needs of the child at that stage. If the majority of the children are at a particular stage, the teacher's interaction and activity planning will reflect this general trend. In the next section I would like to consider the main teaching strategies that support the development of spelling and also to consider what kind of balance needs to be achieved in the context of the child's spelling development.

Strategies to support spelling

The main spelling strategies include the following: kinaesthetic, phonic/alphabetic, visual, and semantic. Kinaesthetic strategies support the motor skills and spatial skills necessary for standard spelling. Finger drawing the alphabet in the sand is a kinaesthetic strategy, as is the attention to appropriate letter formation and pen/pencil control. The physical movements of the hand act as a way of supporting the memory of particular word and letter shapes.

Phonic/alphabetic strategies develop the child's understanding of the alphabet. It is important that the letter names are used right from the start. The child needs to be made aware that letter names and their associated sounds are two quite different concepts. Focusing on the initial letter of words is another commonly used phonic/alphabetic strategy.

Visual strategies focus on the visual memory. Look, cover, write, check is a whole-word visual memory strategy, as are games such as word lotto. An emphasis on word structure is another example of the use of visual strategies. The teacher helps the pupil to become aware of the limitations of phonics by illustrating the way that common letter patterns regularly do not sound the same.

Semantic strategies emphasize the importance of meaning. I would describe the encouragement to invent spellings as a global semantic strategy, as it expects the child to focus on meaning in order to relieve some of the constraints of the transcription skills. For older children, the awareness of words that sound the same but have different meanings is another semantic strategy. Similarly, an emphasis on whole texts, whole sentences and whole words as opposed to excessive focus on individual letters or pairs of letters is a semantic strategy. It is interesting to note that the sound of a letter can only be identified accurately if the meaning of the word is known. What sound does the letter 'E' make? What sound does it make in the word 'read'? What if 'read' is used like this: 'A few days ago I read a book'? The use of dictionaries to check appropriate meanings is another example of a semantic spelling strategy.

Teachers need to consider the emphasis they place on kinaesthetic, phonic/alphabetic, visual and semantic strategies. This decision is informed by two significant considerations: the needs of the individual child during interaction; and the needs of the majority of children in the class. Figure 4.8 illustrates a possible way of balancing the four spelling strategies according to the developmental stage of the child.

At the mark making stage the teacher will focus mainly on phonic/alphabetic and semantic strategies. The emphasis on meaningful and purposeful writing and the development of invented spelling give the appropriate weight

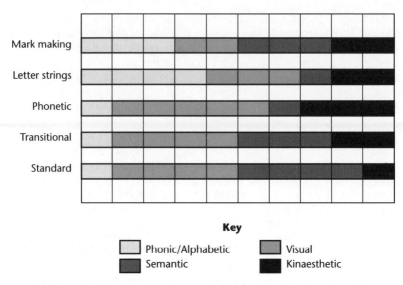

Figure 4.8 Anticipated balance of teacher interaction strategies: spelling

to semantic strategies. This is coupled with regular work on the letters of the alphabet and some of the sounds, and the use of poetry, rhyme and songs. Work on pencil control supports the kinaesthetic sense, and word lists, word games and memorization support the visual strategies.

Once the child or group is using letter strings, the balance changes. It is hoped that most children will feel motivated and confident enough to express themselves, and see a genuine purpose for their writing. This is reflected in the smaller weighting given to semantic strategies. The increased emphasis on phonic/alphabetic reflects the need to encourage the child to use their developing phonetic knowledge to experiment with spellings. Visual strategies mainly target the concept of word. Cutting sentences into words, making collections of similar words, understanding word spaces, playing word games etc. all support this.

The confident phonetic speller needs to gradually understand the limitations of phonic strategies. Many English words require a good visual memory. The teacher develops the child's understanding of word structure, serial probability (the expected order of letters, for example a word is unlikely to start 'qa', unless it is *qadi*!), common letter patterns, silent letters etc. The child becomes good at breaking words into syllables, morphemes and other meaningful units.

As the child passes through the transitional stage towards standard spelling, phonic and kinaesthetic strategies will be used only occasionally to help with some problem words. (For example, when we check a spelling by writing different versions on a scrap of paper, the look and the feel of writing the word sometimes helps us remember the correct version.) The child begins to identify their own set of problem words, and they devise strategies for remembering. The dictionary becomes a more useful tool, as does the spell check on a computer. However, the problem with homophones in this context still requires support through strategies that emphasize semantics. Children at this stage will face choices between a range of possible visual letter patterns for a given word. The teacher helps them remember the correct patterns for the words that they use.

The stages of spelling development provide teachers with a structure that they can use to monitor children's progress. When the stages are matched with the teacher's interaction strategies and their activity planning, a balance can be found that ensures that spelling is tackled in a realistic way. The chapter has examined the practice of invented spelling from the perspectives of children's writing and the balance of the teacher's interaction. The final part of the chapter looks at other published material related to the teaching and learning of spelling.

Theory and research

Perhaps the most important study on spelling was the seminal work of Margaret Peters (1985), whose book *Spelling Caught or Taught* (originally published in 1967) extended some of the debates to do with teacher intervention as opposed to facilitation. She argued that spelling is a skill 'caught' by many, but one which needs direct instruction for a significant number of pupils. One of the important aspects of her work was the range of strategies she identified as being necessary if pupils were to become good spellers. Significantly, she challenged notions of spelling as a mainly auditory skill and emphasized the visual strategies. Peters extended her early categorization of spelling strategies to include kinaesthetic strategies, and suggested that children should be taught words kinaesthetically and visually.

In addition to stressing the vital importance of 'visual reference' in spelling, Cripps and Peters (1990) make the important distinction between phonics for reading and phonics for spelling. They suggest that phonic strategies for reading are more valuable than phonic strategies for spelling. The necessity to 'decode' while reading is replaced by the necessity to 'encode' while writing. The two concepts are related but have distinct differences. When children are trying to spell a word, the phonic strategy presents them with a range of possibilities. For example, if a child is trying to spell 'bear' they may try 'bair'; they will only find the correct spelling if their visual and semantic knowledge is utilized.

Mudd's (1994) book *Effective Spelling: A Practical Guide for Teachers* is a thorough and recent review of the teaching and learning of spelling. She makes the important point that generalizations are more valuable than rules. Rules imply that they are fixed and always correct; generalizations suggest that the concept is generally true but that there may be exceptions. Mudd describes the popular 'magic E' rule where the E at the end of the word lengthens the vowel sound. The problem with treating this as a rule is that there are many exceptions. However, by thinking of it as a generalization and communicating this distinction to children, you are encouraging them to seek out the words which prove or disprove it. The other popular rule is ' "I" before "E" except after "C" when the sound is "EE" '. The rule is perhaps helpful in two ways: it can be used to illustrate to children that language does have rules but that they are complex;

and, most rules have exceptions, and the search for these exceptions can help children to recognize the limitations of strict rule-based approaches to spelling.

The importance of early handwriting instruction including letter formation is also supported by Mudd. She recommends the use of 'multi-sensory routines' where children 'trace the letter in the air or on their desks' and where 'sand-trays, clay, plasticine, pastry, chalk and blackboards are all useful in reinforcing letter shapes'. Mudd also suggests that the practice of using pictures to identify children's coat hooks in the cloakroom perhaps needs some re-evaluation. The use of the children's names alone can be an important early contribution to the notions of letter formation and the function of upper and lower case letters. The importance of understanding the alphabet and the writing of the child's name is also stressed by Tizard (1993). Tizard's study tried to identify early literacy skills that were the best predictors of success at age 11.

> A finding which surprises many teachers is that the best predictor of reading achievement at ages seven and eleven years was the number of letters the children could identify, and their skill at writing their names and copying words, at the nursery stage. Identifying letters and handwriting skills were independent predictors of later reading achievement.
>
> (Tizard 1993: 78)

Peters (1991) suggested that 'children can be seen passing through clear developmental stages'. Peters, LINC (1992) and Temple *et al.* (1982) all cite the work of Gentry (1981) for their evidence of developmental stages for spelling. Gentry outlined the following categories:

1 **Pre-communicative:** a child knows that the symbols create a message and have meaning. The symbols used, however, may be invented.
2 **Semi-phonetic:** a child is beginning to understand that letters have sounds. Often words appear to be abbreviated, or there is a combination of abbreviated forms and pictures, suggesting a merging of stages one and two.
3 **Phonetic:** children operate on a sound symbol basis which may violate the accepted letter strings of English. Gentry cites spellings such as 'monstr' and 'ate' (eighty).
4 **Transitional:** moves beyond the sound–symbol correspondence principle. Children use spellings that reflect the accepted letter strings of English and are therefore beginning to appreciate the visual aspects of spelling.
5 **Correct:** the emergence of the abilities of the fully competent speller, viz.:
   (i)   the use of visual strategies
   (ii) an understanding of the basic spelling patterns of English
   (iii) a knowledge of word structure
   (iv) the use of a large 'automatic' spelling vocabulary
   (v)   the ability to distinguish homonyms (words spelled the same way but with different meanings, e.g. lead (verb) and lead (metal)) and homophones (words with the same sound but different meanings and different spellings, e.g. there and their or bare and bear.)

(LINC 1992: 146)

Gentry's categories described a developmental process; however, two of the categories could have been more appropriately named. The label 'pre-communicative' has some implicit negativity. If a child can 'create a message', they are undoubtedly communicating. As I suggested in Chapter 2, pre-school children come to school with a vast knowledge of literacy; this is often translated into mark making and role-play in the nursery. Given an interested adult, most children can be encouraged to read what they have written. Kress (1982) suggested that regarding children's spelling attempts as absolute errors and created without thought could limit the child's range of thinking and confidence. In the light of this idea, Gentry's stage 5 'Correct' might have been better named as 'Standard', bearing in mind that children's early spellings often demonstrate consistent logical thinking. Invented spellings might more helpfully be seen as positive signs of systematic thought and trial and error, rather than incorrect.

Unlike Peters, Hepburn (1991) derived her category set from the spelling errors of pupils rather than by looking at competent spellers. The aim of the research was to work on a system to enable teachers to:

1 Identify the specific types of errors the child is making.
2 Focus on common errors.
3 Devise strategies specifically catering to the problem.

(Hepburn 1991: 33)

It is not clear how the category set was compiled, but the categories do offer a useful framework for thinking about children's spelling errors. The category set was described as follows:

Morphological	the child makes an error through lack of morphological understanding of the word structure.
Articulation	the child's articulation of the word causes a phonetic error.
Generalization	the child's search for rules causes over generalization.
Homophone confusion	words that sound the same but look different cause an error.
Doubled consonant	doubles a consonant unnecessarily.
Single consonant	forgets that consonant should be doubled.
Shortened word	
Reversal	letters are reversed.
Silent letter	
Spacing error	concept of words and spaces.

(Hepburn 1991: 33)

The idea that articulation causes spelling errors is important. If phonic strategies are over-emphasized, individual pupils' articulation will affect the way they attempt spellings. Teachers who try to suggest that there are fixed ways of pronouncing phonemes may experience difficulties with pupils who use their own accent in order to sound words out. Hepburn goes on to offer activities that might support spelling development in the areas that are weak as identified by the categorization. For example, if the child has problems with silent letters, Hepburn recommends a number of strategies or activities:

1 Use visually similar words as a way of remembering the problem word.
2 Build lists of words that contain the same silent letter.
3 Point out silent letters in words during shared reading sessions with big books.
4 During writing conference, draw the child's attention to words with silent letters.

Donald Graves (1983) believed that the emphasis should be on spelling to communicate. He described a child called Jeremy who was 95 per cent accurate when asked to write initial sounds, final sounds, blends and digraphs. But when writing a 100-word piece of writing, typically he would misspell 10 to 15 words. Jeremy was working within a process as opposed to a decontextualized activity; this made much greater demands on his ability. When teachers count the number of correct spellings and keep a record over time, they can build up a simple profile of a child's spelling development. Some teachers have found that the genre of a piece of writing has a direct impact on spelling. If children are writing in an unfamiliar genre or one which uses a range of unfamiliar words, they are more likely to make spelling errors.

Graves also categorized the development of spelling, but in a different way to Gentry. Graves's categorization was mainly alphabetic:

STAGE 1 –	Use of initial consonant	G
STAGE 2 –	Initial and final consonant	GS
STAGE 3 –	Initial, final and interior consonant	GRS
STAGE 4 –	Initial, final, and interior consonants, and vowel place holder. Vowel is incorrect but in correct position	GRES
STAGE 5 –	Child has full spelling of the word, with final components from visual memory systems and better vowel discrimination	GRASS

(Graves 1983: 184)

Graves did include the visual aspects of spelling development in his last category, but there was no mention of kinaesthetics or the special problems of homophones.

In this chapter I have suggested that the process approach requires the children to use invented spelling and the teacher to utilize a range of teacher interaction strategies. The process approach emphasizes the development of composition, but teachers are constantly faced with decisions concerning the best ways of supporting transcription, and spelling development in particular. A necessary direct classroom focus on spelling, informed by research, need not detract from the compositional process. The teacher needs to balance the interaction during writing conference so that spelling is supported when appropriate. Mudd (1994) and Graves (1983) acknowledge that spelling instruction is difficult during writing workshop. However, the interaction with children during writing conference helps the teacher to see general developments that can be supported by set spelling tasks at different times during the week in addition to the support given during the workshop.

FIVE

Interaction

The process approach is an ideal vehicle for individualized teaching. Children are encouraged to follow their interests through a relatively open framework. The recording of these interests reveals much about their strengths and weaknesses as a writer. The teacher is then able to pitch their interaction appropriately for the individual. It is an opportunity for child centred learning and for differentiation clearly based on the children's needs.

Teachers who use the process approach can develop sophisticated interaction skills. They become perceptive observers, with the behaviour that they observe serving to develop their own understanding of the teaching and learning process. By being good at 'kid watching' they learn to teach better. The range of writing that will be taking place during writing workshop or through emergent writing will mean that the teacher needs to be flexible and adept at responding to a range of compositional and transcriptional demands.

In order to examine the nature of interaction, this chapter describes some research that I carried out. The research focused on the work of three teachers; all three were working in primary schools, Carol and Keith in mainstream schooling and Sarah supporting deaf children in a mainstream primary school. The research focused on the teachers' reflections on their teaching of writing. Each teacher chose one child and wrote their reflections concerning their interaction with the child. The interaction took place during writing conference. For the purpose of the research, writing conference referred to one-to-one interaction between teacher and child where the child's writing was the focus. This definition of writing conference was broader than the one I specify in Chapter 1 of this book.

The first part of the chapter gives a general description of the contexts that the individual teachers were working in. This section includes an outline of the kinds of task that they chose to reflect on and the main focus of their interaction at that time. The next section identifies six significant areas of the teachers' interaction; this is concluded with a diagram that illustrates the links between the categories and the issues that these links raise.

I chose to focus on teacher interaction partly because I felt that much useful research had been carried out that looked at parents and children in the home. Single child case studies such as Bissex (1980) have had a significant impact on teachers, as they have given rich pictures of the developmental characteristics of children's writing. However, these studies have tended to focus on parents and the home rather than teachers. I wanted to illuminate some of the important work that I felt went on during writing conference that is often hidden to the outside observer.

I also felt that much research into teaching and learning had not examined the rationales or aims that were behind the practical and physical manifestations of the primary teacher's work. There are a number of large scale studies that have looked at teacher interaction, but these have often concentrated on the surface features of interaction and were limited in their ability to look below the surface.

Once a fortnight the teachers wrote their reflections about their interaction with the chosen child onto a pro-forma. The style of the pro-forma had been developed during a pilot study. It was divided into two columns, the first column entitled 'What did the child do?' and the second column 'What did I do and why?' As I received each pro-forma I carried out some early analysis and then interviewed the teacher to clarify and cross-check the reflections that they had recorded. This process of cross-checking – or participant validation – was designed to enhance the validity of the data and its early analysis.

The research developed three in-depth case studies that revealed some of the aims and strategies that the teachers used over the year with the child they had chosen. By comparing the three case studies it was possible to see aspects of their practice that were similar in spite of the unique context that each teacher worked in. By looking at these comparisons I found it was also possible to compare them with my own experiences as a primary teacher. I hope that the experiences that are described will also have resonance for other teachers.

The three teachers

The teachers' own descriptions of their school contexts influenced the following accounts.

Keith worked in a large Victorian inner city first school with children who were predominantly British Asian; he taught a Year 4 class. He organized his classroom to support language development by having various classroom areas. The carpet area was used for class discussion, and there were books on shelves around this area. Reading and writing activities occurred throughout the classroom, and the children were trained to decide on their own groupings and seating. He had various writing resources available for the children, including a mixture of pens, pencils, papers, colouring equipment etc. He had one large area where most of his teacher directed tasks took place. The other areas were arranged in varying sizes, seating from five to ten children. He decided to choose an 8-year-old British Asian boy as the context for his reflections whom he was curious to learn more about.

Carol worked in a large urban infant school, again with children who were predominantly British Asian. Carol had curriculum area bays where resources for the curriculum area concerned were arranged near the bay or area. In her language area she had a wide range of resources including dictionaries, word cards, tape recorder, bookmaking, 'Breakthrough' sentence tracks etc. The other areas of her classroom included a number area, art area, investigation area, and a large carpet area with books and construction apparatus. Role-play happened elsewhere in the school due to lack of space in the classrooms. She grouped the children roughly by their ability in English language skills, but at other times children were encouraged to choose peers to work with. She chose a 6-year-old British Asian girl whom she felt she had a good relationship with and whom she thought would show significant progress.

Sarah worked in various classrooms and a deaf unit which was part of a Victorian state primary school. The school was situated in a semi-rural coastal area with a significant number of children from the local council estate. The school had all white British children. Sarah alternated between supporting her children in ordinary lessons and withdrawing them for individual work. The withdrawal room was set up as a normal working classroom with the addition of special equipment for the teaching of deaf children such as hearing aids, remote microphones, speech trainers etc. The displays represented the learning needs of the children and were used as a teaching resource. She chose a 9-year-old boy who had been profoundly deaf since birth. She was particularly interested in discovering more about his writing development over the course of the year.

In order to give an idea of the kinds of reflection that the teachers made, I include one complete pro-forma from each teacher. For the purpose of this book I have removed the columns, but the content of the text remains the same. One of Keith's pro-formas was as follows:

Teacher (T): 'Tell me what you've done.' – Opening question – allows W to read or re-tell.

Child (C): Reads me his writing – story based on reading scheme characters.

T: I point to word 'Kippe' (misspelling) – drawing attention to error.

C: Adds 'r' at end of word to complete spelling correctly. Reads 'Biffs' but has written 'Biff'.

T: 'Biff?' – drawing attention to error without providing any more information.

C: Adds apostrophe and 's'.

T: 'Is there anything else you're not sure is right?' – encouraging W to check his own work.

C: Points to word 'cole' which he reads as 'call'.

T: 'Have another go here.' (I offer some scrap paper – encouraging W to try alternative spellings.)

C: Writes 'cola'.

T: 'That says "cola"' – providing information. 'Do you know how to spell "all"?'

C: 'A-L-L'.
T: 'Do you know how to spell "call" ?' – encouraging W to trans-
        fer/use range of spelling knowledge and understanding.
C: 'C-A-L-L' [Keith's underlining]
T: 'Well done.'

Keith's reflections were characterized by his insistence that the child thought for himself and learned to correct his own errors. He expected him to work out his own spelling mistakes and have the necessary strategies to correct them. In the extract his approach appeared to be successful because the child arrived at the correct spelling. However, rather than just learning the correct spelling, in the course of the interaction the child picked up a series of strategies and understandings related to the development of spelling. Had Keith instructed the child that the word was wrong and told him to correct it, the learning outcome would have been different.

One of Carol's pro-formas looked like this:

T: Group discussion around memories of being little using books and
    photos to illustrate the point. I asked K what she remembered to draw
    some more ideas out and asked her to draw a picture of her memories
    to consolidate the idea prior to writing.
C: K brought picture to me and she told me about it.
T: I asked K to write after listening to her ideas.
C: K went off and did the writing by herself. She came and read it to me.
T: I listened to K and then I read it to her and asked her if she did hear
    any mistakes to get her to focus in on her writing and listen to struc-
    ture of sentences. Together we changed the first sentence.
C: K stood close to me and said she knew what I meant.
T: I then asked her to think about full stops and capitals. She corrected
    them by herself. I praised her for this to get her to acknowledge her
    ability.
C: K said she had finished.
T: I asked her to think of one more idea as K needs encouragement to
    make her writing longer.

The style of Carol's reflections was quite different to Keith's. This difference in style of reflections suggested differences in teaching style. Carol placed a significant emphasis on the social needs of the child. Her reflections made regular reference to the way she built up the child's self-esteem. Her final instruction to the child illustrated one of the common compositional aspects that Carol's interaction focused upon. There was a constant need to extend the length and quality of the children's writing, but at the same time maintaining their self-esteem so they continued to have the motivation to write.

One of Sarah's pro-formas looked like this:

T: I told S that we were going to make a book ... not 'do some writing'
    ... in the hope that I wouldn't get the usual turn off of effort and aver-
    sion to writing. I showed him the book we had read previously and
    told him that we were going to make his own that would be the same.
    I had copied the pictures and showed him the first three pages ... so

as not to overwhelm him. I then asked S to choose which one would go first. In my head I suppose I had a fixed idea of which one he would choose due to the fact that we had already read the book.

C: S did pick the one I was thinking of. I'm not sure how I would have reacted if he had chosen another one ... something I need to consider, i.e. seeing the world from the child's point of view.

T: I then asked him to tell me what was happening in the picture.

C: S signed 'rabbit'.

One of the aims of the activity was to encourage S to use his knowledge of sign to convey information in more detail.

T: So I signed 'who's that?' pointing to the boy in the picture.

C: S signed 'T (for Tim) rabbit holding'.

T: I showed S some words on pieces of paper that contained 'Tim' and 'rabbit'. He retrieved these successfully. I then wrote down the word 'holding'. I didn't ask him to try to write this, didn't want to put him off after his initial success.

C: S stuck on the three words in the order he had signed them. He then signed 'rabbit house in.'

. . .

C: S signed 'r' indicating that he could remember something about the written word rabbit.

T: GREAT! I asked him to write it down on a piece of rough paper. I'm trying to encourage him to take control and ownership of writing.

C: S did this.

The child's deafness meant that much of Sarah's interaction was occupied with the complexities of communicating between sign language, talking, reading and writing. She felt strongly that the linking of these modes would help the child to improve his writing. For all teachers the relationship between the language modes is one that is addressed in a number of ways.

The teachers varied in the extent to which they used the process approach. Often this variation arose because of the ethos of the particular school. The next section examines the nature of the activities that the teachers used, the extent of their use of the process approach, and the primary focus of the writing conference that they chose to reflect upon.

Use of the process approach

Of the three teachers, Keith used the process approach the most. Table 5.1 shows the balance between the process approach (signified by writing workshop) and structured tasks that Keith offered.

The first thing to note about the table showing Keith's writing activities (as with Sarah and Carol) is that it only represents a snapshot of the activities that were taking place during the year. However, some interesting issues did arise. During writing workshop sessions the child chose to write stories for all the writing conferences that Keith chose to reflect upon. He confirmed that many of the children in his class chose story above other forms. The reasons for this choice were unclear. There are four possible explanations:

Table 5.1   Keith's writing activities and interaction focus

Data collection pro-forma	Nature of activity	Primary focus of writing conference
1	Scary story	Extend amount and complexity of writing and improve spelling
2	Writing workshop – story	Improve spelling
3	Writing workshop – story based on reading scheme characters	Develop ability to self-correct
4	Writing workshop – same story, second draft	Improve drafting skills
5	Writing workshop – second story based on reading scheme characters	Raise awareness of issues; using published texts for stimulus in an appropriate way
6	Scientific writing – burning candles covered by glass jars	Use of drafting symbol
7	Diary writing – linked to recording of historical events	Syntax structure
8	Writing workshop – The Monster and the Two Boys	Strategies for checking spellings
9	Writing workshop – The Magic Key	Generating ideas and improving punctuation
10	Writing workshop – second draft of Forest story	Using computer as drafting tool
11	Writing workshop – story	Improve drafting skills
12	Writing workshop – The Magic Key	Improve spelling

1 Stories held a particular significance for the child; they were more interesting and relevant than other forms.
2 Frequent exposure to stories had given the child more confidence to write them himself.
3 As the genre theorists have suggested, perhaps there was too much emphasis on stories in the school as a whole.
4 The choice of form represents a developmental stage, with other forms taking priority later.

The research did not provide enough evidence to make a definitive statement about the reasons for the prevalence of story.

As we see from Table 5.1, Keith set up other genres of writing such as the science writing and the diary writing. He confirmed that throughout the year the use of writing workshop was balanced with a range of set tasks that

Table 5.2   Carol's writing activities and interaction focus

Data collection pro-forma	Nature of activity	Primary focus of writing conference
1	Book written for an imaginary giant titled 'My School'	Ideas for writing
2	PE lesson as stimulus for 'My School' book	Syntax structure
3	Write about assembly for 'My School' book	Use of word card
4	The Sun, Moon and Earth; recall class discussion	Circles for words
5	Christmas story	Initial letter strategy
6	Transfer words from reading book onto alphabetic word card	Positive feedback and encouragement to continue independently
7	Transfer words from reading book into child's dictionary	Gave spellings of words not in reading book that the child wanted to record
8	Description of ice	Use of word card
9	Finding words in dictionary and drawing picture of word	Whole word memory
10	Describing the rooms in child's house for 'My house' book	Independence
11	Cloze procedure – fill in missing words	Collaborative skills
12	Self chosen sections for 'My house' book	Independence
13	Re-enact 'Jack and the Beanstalk'	Directionality
14	My earliest memories	Sentence structure
15	Animals and their homes	Sentence structure

emphasized various genres; however, he still found that story was a particularly popular form.

Carol's list of activities has clear differences from Keith's. In spite of a philosophical commitment to the process approach, Carol found its implementation difficult. In her previous school the ethos had supported process approaches, and this was reflected in the language policy. The school that Carol was working in during the research had a more traditional approach to the teaching of language and literacy. When Carol tried to implement the process approach in her classroom she found that the children's previous

Table 5.3   Sarah's writing activities and interaction focus

Data collection pro-forma	Nature of activity	Primary focus of writing conference
1	Word recognition and sentence structure – words on cards	Syntax
2	Bookmaking with sequence of pictures as stimulus	Understanding of 'to give'
3	Writing in response to story	Links between talking, reading and writing
4	Describe feelings shown in pictures	Computer skills
5	Spelling test and game	Visual memory skills
6	Story writing with choice of books for stimulus	Syntax and word meaning
7	Write examples of print in the environment from book	Prepare for local visit looking at environmental print. Reading prediction skills
8	Role-play with dolls as stimulus	Extending language
9	Comprehension – ing words	Word structure
10	Story writing	Correct sign for 'book'
11	Writing numbers in response to number game	Use of 'before' and 'after'
12	Writing workshop	Developing creativity

experiences made this difficult. They had particular expectations about the way they thought they would be taught. Carol decided to try and change small aspects of the children's experience gradually, and work towards the development of a whole school approach to language and literacy.

Carol chose to reflect on sessions that included language skills work, and again this differed from the sessions that Keith chose to record. In part this represented the different ages of the respective children. However, the choice of session also gave an indication of the individual teaching style. The activities that encouraged the child to collect words and arrange them alphabetically on a word card or personal dictionary were used to develop the child's alphabetic knowledge and memory of certain words. The activities were not completely decontextualized, as the child was encouraged to use her reading book as the source for the words she chose.

The special needs of the child that Sarah was working with meant that there were differences between her approach and those of the other two teachers. However, there were significant similarities in terms of the aims and strategies that she and the other teachers used to encourage writing. At the start of the year Sarah's reflections emphasized the way she focused on quite specific understandings of syntax. She regularly linked the language modes of talking, signing, reading and writing in order to try and consolidate the skills and concepts she was trying to teach. Throughout the year there was a continuum that began with many tightly structured activities that focused on particular skills and understandings and that ended with her final reflections on the writing workshop session that she ran. This gradual development in approach reflected her desire to build on the child's past experiences and to fit in with the ethos of the hearing impaired children's unit. However, she had strong views of how the child's experiences could be improved.

In spite of the differences between the three children and the classroom contexts, there were a number of significant areas of similarity between the teachers' reflections. For example, Sarah's desire to maintain the child's motivation was an aim shared by all three teachers, and this was evident in their reflections. Similarly, Sarah's intention to increase the level of detail that the child used was an aim that the other teachers revealed. Of course the three children who were chosen for the reflections were at different stages of development, and this was reflected in the kind of interaction. However, a number of general categories of interaction emerged that were common to all three teachers.

Interaction categories

The analysis of the teachers' reflections revealed six significant general categories of interaction. During writing conference the teachers' aims for their interaction were regularly focused on these six areas. When I related these categories to my own classroom practice I became aware that there were a number of similarities. It is possible that other teachers may recognize the importance of these areas in their own teaching.

Assess

At the start and during the course of the interaction the teachers regularly made quick assessments of the particular needs that the child had. This ongoing assessment was a recurrent strategy, and it helped the teacher to be responsive at all times to the child, their writing and their development. This was not a formalized assessment but more a way of reflecting upon the child's progress at that moment. This ability to couple sensitive observation with constructive support is a vital skill.

> T: 'That's not a real word, listen – heard' (I say the word emphasizing the 'r' sound. Helping him to use phonic cues to assist in spelling).
> C: He writes 'heard'.
> T: 'You think that's right?' – Challenging him, forcing him to assess how sure he is.
> C: He writes herd.
> T: 'No! The last one was right.' I explain I was seeing if he knew he was right.

Not only did Keith assess the child's knowledge of the spelling, but he encouraged the child to reflect on his own self-correction ability.

Self-esteem

The teachers regularly aimed to support the children's self-esteem. Throughout their reflections on their interaction all three teachers indicated the strategies they used to support the child's self-esteem. Often this was through the positive feedback they offered the child. The teachers' reflections documented one of the difficulties that they faced when teaching writing. They wanted to focus on the development of writing; however, it was clear that the child's social needs could not be ignored. The teachers recognized that the child's feelings about the activity or their feelings about the aspect of writing that they were receiving support for, were inseparable from the curriculum demands. If the child loses confidence ('I can't do it!') and/or motivation, the chances for learning are greatly reduced.

> C: K went off and completed the work without using her word book.
> T: I praised K highly for the sentences and the full stops. I didn't ask her to look at capitals as I felt she had achieved a lot and it would be negative.
> T: I then went over [to the child].
> C: S attempted to read the words under each picture.
> T: I had given him one which I knew he would be able to attempt.

In the first extract Carol gave the child positive feedback that identified the sentence structure and the full stops. She also supported the child's self-esteem by deciding not to ask the child to correct the capital letters, as she felt that this might have decreased the child's motivation on this occasion. Sarah also used this kind of technique for supporting the child's self-esteem. Her awareness of the child's needs and development allowed her to offer support materials that she felt would help the child to succeed. She anticipated potential failure and increased the child's chances for success, recognizing that this early support for his self-esteem would pay dividends later on.

Independence

This category of interaction aims was particularly important. It described the teachers' reflections that showed how they developed their children's independence. Independence was seen to be a positive characteristic of the children's development. The category existed at a number of different levels. General independence was seen to be necessary because it meant that the child could learn more quickly by not relying on too much teacher or peer support. This included the ability to select suitable resources for a task. Specific independence revealed itself, for example, in the ability to invent spellings. This confidence to take risks and not be afraid of making mistakes helped the child to learn by solving their own problems and generating their own hypotheses and useful generalizations.

C: Reads [his writing]. The entry concerns what happened to him that morning. He reads 'Don't go to school now' when he has written 'don't go to now'.

T: 'Where does it say school?' – pointing out an error but <u>requiring him to identify it.</u>

Keith gave the child some guidance in that he implied that there was an error. But instead of simply giving the child the correct answer or telling the child what the mistake was, he encouraged the child to independently locate the error. This developed the child's ability to spot mistakes and gave him the specific information that he required.

Learning links

The three teachers developed links between the various aspects of the teaching and learning process. Writing was often linked with the other language modes of talking and reading in order to consolidate learning and to help the child understand the interconnected nature of language. Sometimes this was implicit in the reflections. For example, the teachers would encourage the children to read their writing and they would then engage in discussion about it. The culmination of the discussion would often be recommendations for improvement of the writing.

T: I had been writing words in the sand with Simon.

C: He expressed with gesture that he liked the feel of the sand.

T: <u>I gave him the new sign, the spoken and written word</u> and asked him to learn it as one of his weekly spellings.

In this example Sarah started with the kinaesthetic sense of touch by encouraging the child to experience the letter shape by drawing in the sand. As she did on many occasions, this was followed by reference to signing, speaking and writing in the hope that the range of modes would consolidate the learning. The teachers also used activities and strategies to consolidate learning by relating present activities to past or future activities. This helped the children reflect on the nature of learning as a developmental process.

Composition

In the study, the analysis turned to an in-depth look at composition and transcription. The result of some of this analysis is illustrated in the chapter on composition (Chapter 3). However, in this chapter I offer extracts from the basic raw data that illustrate the teachers' reflections in these areas. Composition described the authorship issues or content issues that the teacher encouraged the child to develop.

Child (C):   Waqaas was making the second entry in his diary. (The class were keeping diaries as part of the current topic – Tudors and Stuarts).

Teacher (T): I looked over his shoulder and saw the date 1666. 'This is meant to be about <u>your</u> life <u>now</u>. What happened to you today, this morning?' – helping Waqaas to understand this type of writing – content and purpose.

C: 'I didn't come to school. I had a headache.'

T: 'Write about that.' – giving a concrete suggestion for content.

[Child] writes; I go elsewhere.

Later:

T: 'What have you written?' – checking on content, encouraging Waqaas to check on content.

C: Reads. The entry concerns what happened to him that morning. He reads 'Don't go to school now' [but] he has written 'don't go to now'.

T: 'Where does it say school?' – pointing out an error but requiring him to identify it.

C: Rubs out 'now' and replaces it with 'school'.

T: 'Does that say what you want now?' – encouraging him to check content/meaning.

During the period of interaction illustrated by the extract Keith had decided to focus on the composition of Waqaas' writing. Initially Keith helped the child to understand the overall focus for the activity. The misunderstanding by the child was partly a result of the different ways that Punjabi and English reflect the concept of time. The activity was particularly demanding because later it involved a comparison between Waqaas' present diary with diary entries from the Tudor period. Keith emphasized the child's role in redrafting his own work and understanding the necessity for redrafting. The focus on composition moved from whole text level to sentence level and towards the end of the conference, to word level.

Transcription

The teachers supported the children's development of the secretarial and presentation skills of their writing. The data from the study showed that the majority of the teachers' reflections in this category were devoted to spelling.

T: I asked K to look in her reading book and find words to put under each letter in the [her] dictionary to encourage her to look at initial letters.

C: K came to me when she couldn't find a word to go under a letter.

T: I said 'not to worry, go onto the next'. The idea wasn't to find one for each letter necessarily.

C: K came to me to ask for spellings of words not in her reading book.

T: I gave them to her by spelling out the word to her. To encourage her enthusiasm for finding words and encourage her to remember the word and not just copy.

Carol's interaction at this point focused on transcription and specifically on spelling. She usefully contextualized the activity for the child by encouraging her to use words from her reading book. Having read the book and perhaps discussed it with others, the further focus on spellings is more meaningful.

The writing interaction framework

Part of the analysis of the data involved looking at the links between the categories. It was important to consider the relationships between the categories and how these relationships were related to the practice of the teachers.

By looking at the categories as a whole and considering the links between them it was possible to create an illustrative framework (Figure 5.1). The framework focused on how the interaction categories were related in the context of writing conference. By presenting the framework it is my intention that teachers will be able to reflect upon their own interaction during writing conference to assess the significance of the categories and the links that exist between them.

The picture as a whole represents some of the conflicting demands that the teaching and learning context make on the teacher. The primary aim of the teacher is to develop the child's ability as a writer. In order to do this they have to support and take account of various other factors that can either impede or complement the learning objectives. These learning objectives exist at three levels:

1 The teacher has a set of pedagogic beliefs that have been accumulated through the process of professional development. These beliefs determine how the teacher structures the activities and the teaching and learning context.
2 At another level the teacher sets specific learning objectives that are built into the activity planning.
3 Finally, during the interaction itself the teacher has learning aims and teaching strategies that help them teach the child.

The arrangement of the categories in the diagram reflects the complex demands that are made on the teacher during interaction. As an illustration

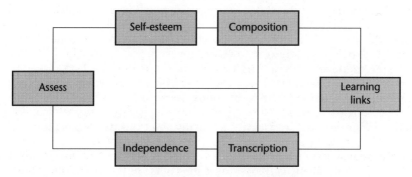

Figure 5.1 The links between the interaction categories

of this, let us consider a child who needs help with his writing. Stuart is working on a story about a football team. He is an independent worker who sometimes verges on being rather a loner. He has quite low self-esteem in spite of the fact that he is usually on task and works to the best of his ability. In conversation with Stuart's mother the teacher has found out that his low self-esteem has in part been created by the difficulties he has at home because of his brother, who has special needs. The teacher feels that the compositional aspects of Stuart's story are quite good. He is writing with enthusiasm but needs support with his spelling.

> T: 'I enjoyed the part where the YMCA team got to the top of the league.'
> S: 'I thought of that because our team is always at the bottom.'
> T: 'Mmm. Have you checked the spellings yet?'
> S: 'No.'
> T: 'OK let's read it together.'
> S: 'I didn't know how to spell league.'
> T: 'Yes that's a difficult word. Like lots of English words it doesn't look like it sounds. All the letters you used are correct ['lege']. Do you know the other two letters?'
> S: 'Is there an A in it?'
> T: 'Yes there is, and a U. Like this . . . Do you know any other words that end "gue"?'
> S: 'ummm . . . argue.'
> T: 'Yes!'

In the example the teacher's interaction would be reflected primarily in two categories of the interaction framework. She built up the child's *self-esteem* by giving focused positive feedback and she tackled one of the *transcription* elements through their discussion about the spelling of 'league'.

Assessment is often a starting point for teachers. For example, at the beginning of a year the teacher gets to know the strengths of the children. However, assessment is also an ongoing process. At the beginning of a writing conference the teacher finds out where the child is in the process before offering support. Also, the developing relationship between child and teacher, and sensitive interaction during writing conference, help the teacher to assess the child's immediate needs and intervene in a productive way. During interaction the affective needs of the child – represented by *self-esteem* and *independence* – are balanced by the pedagogical and curriculum demands represented by the other categories. This reflects the need to understand the social needs of the child if curriculum learning is to be maximized.

Learning links are often a culmination of the teaching and learning process. Having learnt a concept or skill, the teacher wants to know whether the learning can be transferred to other situations. Sometimes this consolidation takes place through specific activities, at other times it is part of the interaction. In addition, the teacher is constantly, implicitly and explicitly, linking the modes of writing, reading and talking. The particular context will determine the balance that is attached to the various categories. For most children, support will be given in all the categories over the course of the year. Some children will require greater emphasis in certain areas depending on their development.

In this chapter I have illustrated a snapshot of the work of three teachers over the course of a year. Their work illustrates the complexities and opportunities that exist for teaching and learning during writing conference. The six categories that illuminate aspects of their interaction aims are perhaps common to other teachers. One of the implications following from the study is that perhaps English teaching policy should take account of the full range of issues that teachers have to deal with in the classroom context. For teachers the implications are to do with the necessity to reflect on the nature of interaction and to consider the kind of balance they achieve between the various demands that are made.

| | | SIX

| | | Recording language development

The recording of language development is a complex process that has resulted in a wide array of tools and formats for the purpose. Often there is confusion between the terms 'recording' and 'assessing', in addition to some natural overlap between the two concepts. It is not within the scope of this chapter to describe and compare the differing formats, nor do I intend to look in detail at summative assessments of children's progress. Instead, the chapter will focus particularly on naturalistic methods of recording children's language development.

I have argued throughout the book that the process approach is a flexible system that encourages children to take control of their writing. The outcomes of such an approach reflect the diversity of individuals in the class. As we compare these individuals we begin to see similarities and patterns. These patterns enable us to predict developmental characteristics, and they offer the opportunity for teaching and learning to be closely linked with a thorough understanding of the children's needs.

The reality of teachers as reflective practitioners who base their teaching on perceptive observation of their pupils is not easy to achieve. It is particularly difficult if written observations are not made. In fact, without written observations it is very difficult to reflect in sufficient depth on the complex issues to do with teaching and learning that the teacher faces. When teachers do make written observations, these quickly build up into a substantial amount of information that can enable the teacher to reflect on the needs of children and areas for their own professional development.

This chapter focuses particularly on adaptations to the Primary Language Record (Barrs *et al.* 1989) and record keeping that is influenced by such approaches. The decision to focus particularly on the Primary Language Record (PLR) is based on my opinion that it is a particularly effective system for making records when using the process approach. In order to illustrate the benefits of naturalistic recording systems, I describe in depth my own experience using the PLR in one school. Additionally, the work of another school's approach to the recording of reading is described. By looking in depth at the work of teachers I hope to illustrate that decisions made on the choice of recording systems can have implications beyond the effective recording of children's progress.

The chapter looks closely at the recording of parent/teacher conferences that focused on language and literacy; it also addresses the recording of reading. The section on the recording of writing is somewhat shorter, as the aim of the chapter is to explore some generic principles for the recording of language which are applicable to all three language modes. The recording of writing is also evident in other chapters of the book, and provides evidence to support a number of the ideas that I put forward. The chapter concludes with an analysis of another school's approach to the recording of reading.

The use of the Primary Language Record

Shortly after the 'consultation' for the original National Curriculum, the Task Group on Assessment and Testing recommended a model for record keeping which was epitomized by the PLR. This was seen as a thorough, professional and above all useful tool for recording children's achievements in the development of language/English. Not only did the record give meaningful information about children's development, but it also offered naturalistic data which could be analysed to provide important information on the success of teaching and learning in primary schools. Recently, the style of the observation sheets of the PLR has influenced the Standard Assessment Task (SAT) guidelines. The 1996 SAT materials contained a framework for observing children's reading behaviour that looked similar to the reading samples framework of the PLR.

When schools adopt the process approach, the style of record keeping needs to be in line with the philosophies that underpin the approach. The most useful records are based on the observations that teachers make of children at work. These combine the teacher's current knowledge of the child with their rigorous observation skills. It follows that these observations are best recorded in a format that allows some flexibility within structured guidelines, and that the format is suitable for text, i.e. written comments. It is for these reasons that I believe the PLR is such a useful tool.

The Centre for Language in Primary Education (CLPE) designed the PLR and it was thoroughly piloted in a wide range of London schools. Since its introduction there have been criticisms that it is rather time consuming to implement in full. I think this is a reasonable criticism of the record as a whole, but the criticism does not preclude the use of individual sections, so schools and organizations can tailor the record to their own needs.

In this section of the chapter I will show how the Primary Language Record can be modified to suit a school's individual needs while maintaining the spirit of the philosophies which underpin it. The process of using and adapting the PLR is in stark contrast to the use of National Curriculum tick-lists. Although Sir Ron Dearing reported that the use of comprehensive tick-lists was inappropriate, the practice still continues. The PLR serves teachers in the understanding of the children they teach, in addition to the potential of developing a better understanding of the teacher's role and the school's role in the teaching and learning situation.

While I was language coordinator for an inner city school, we developed the use of the Primary Language Record as the culmination of an intense period of whole school language development. The children at the school were predominantly of Asian origin, and the record is one of the few which explicitly highlights some of the issues which confront teachers of bilingual children. However, it was the underlying educational philosophies of the record which attracted me to it more than any other consideration. The fact that these are articulated in some detail in the PLR handbook also marks the record as a package with substance.

The record has two parts. The buff coloured formal document is a summative record of the child's development in language which the teacher fills in. Some of the innovative features include a record of the child's views about their own progress, a record of the parents' views, whether the child was summer born as this has implications for the length of time spent in nursery and reception, and information on the child's other languages. The second part is an observation framework which the teacher uses throughout the year to provide information for the final record. Although many teachers keep notes on children's achievements, this is a useful format for ensuring that the most important aspects are recorded. I found that the introduction of both sections of the document at one time would have been unmanageable; therefore it was decided to introduce those aspects which were most appropriate in terms of the school's development.

The most significant part of the formal document is the 'Record of discussion between child's parent(s) and class teacher' (for an analysis of teacher/pupil talk during 'child conferences' see Stierer 1995). Although the need to involve parents more in the education of their children has been an aim for schools for some time, in practice this can be difficult to achieve. Standard parent evenings and yearly reports tend to be rather one-way, with the teacher summarizing their opinions of the child's progress. The school I was working for had a well established programme of home visits where all teachers visited each child's home once a year. These visits were established to improve contact with the parents, some of whom felt unable to visit the school for a variety of reasons. I felt the meetings fulfilled an important social function, but lacked focus and educational purpose. The majority of teachers agreed that some form of recording would be useful provided it was made clear to the parents why we were making notes. The teachers also requested some kind of framework in order to ensure the best use was being made of the time available. Figure 6.1 shows our adaptation of the Primary Language Record. The bold type shows the prompt that was available for teachers doing home visits. Next to this I have summarized some of the school's findings which influenced our approaches to teaching and learning.

The school's emphasis on home visits meant that the 'record of discussion between child's parent(s) and class teacher' was much more detailed than in the PLR. This reflected the school's tradition of developing good relationships with the parents over a number of years.

Figure 6.1   Parent/teacher discussion framework

Parents' concerns
- *This space is used to record any questions or concerns parents have concerning the language development of their child in terms of talking and listening, reading and writing*

All staff were keen to empower parents, therefore it was decided to initiate the visit with an open agenda where parents could voice any immediate concerns. This was seen as a smoother transition from unstructured interviews to structured ones. Parents were very interested in the general progress of their child, particularly in literacy. 'How is she doing?' was a common question, as was 'How is he at reading and writing?' Regularly there were other issues which they wanted to discuss, such as the child's eating habits, medical concerns, relationship with peers or current events featured in the news.

Talking and listening

• **Languages spoken at home/community**	This section was used to check school information on languages the bilingual children used and the context for their use. Occasionally the teachers discovered dialects or variations of the languages they didn't know about. For example, Hinko was a dialect from the north west of Pakistan which the school wasn't aware of.
• **Importance of using home/community language at school**	Most parents felt that it was a good thing that children were encouraged to use all the languages at their disposal. However, there was a significant minority who felt that English should be the only language of the classroom and that their children would learn it quicker if this was the case.
• **Social groups, e.g. sport, recreation, religious**	Many of the bilingual children went on to Mosque or Temple schools in the late afternoon. The teaching methods were often different from schools, and this provoked discussions on how the two approaches could be understood and reconciled.
• **Play and games**	'Proper' work was seen as reading, writing and maths. Play was not seen as particularly important for the child's education.

Reading

• **In more than one language?**	Many children learnt large chunks of the Koran through rote learning and chanting.

Figure 6.1 (continued)

They could read the Arabic word-perfect but seemingly without understanding. This created tension with approaches to reading which emphasized the semantic nature of text.

• **Interest in print, e.g. TV, food labels, signs, letters, cards, news, magazines**

Although environmental print became an academic issue for the teachers, parents tended to see it as utilitarian and not of much relevance.

• **Interest in books/comics. Library?**

Most children had texts at home, although the quality of these depended on the financial situation of the family concerned. Older brothers and sisters sometimes took the children to the local library if it wasn't too far away, although this was quite rare.

• **Sharing books with child**

Unfortunately, many parents lacked the confidence to share books with their children. Often they felt that if they couldn't read English, the process of sharing a book would be useless. However, older siblings often did share with younger members of the family.

• **Changes in ability**

This was an important question for the teachers and parents alike. The vociferous minority's views often wielded disproportionate power when staff discussed teaching approaches. The evidence from the visits showed that parents were by and large happy. If there were parents who were concerned, teachers were able to address their needs.

Writing
• **Availability and use of pens, pencils and paper/workbooks**

Most of the children had access to writing resources periodically. A common problem was younger siblings who tended to tear up and eat writing they tried to produce.

• **Pictures, written marks or attempted writing**

Parents were sometimes pleased that the marks that their children made had so much meaning in them. Sometimes they found they were so busy that they didn't give the writing the attention it needed.

• **Languages written; copied or invented**

Recording writing

The work with parents during the parent–teacher conference helped us to examine a number of issues for the recording of reading and writing. When recording writing we felt that it was important to keep in mind the fact that the child's writing itself offered an important opportunity for record keeping. The use of portfolios of children's writing has become quite common; however, the collection of the writing alone does not provide the necessary context and analysis that enables the teacher to make decisions on the child's development.

The important contribution of marking, or written responses to children's writing, should not be overlooked in relation to record keeping. The teacher's written comments should refer to specific examples that were positive about the writing and offer specific guidance on how the writing could be improved. This issue is tied in with the school's approach to marking. The following example shows how the school responded to an inspection comment by agreeing a 'common marking policy'.

'Good' at the bottom of a piece of work conveys little to the child, but a more specific comment about one aspect of the piece that was good is likely to help build confidence in the child.

Common marking policy and specific intervention
When we respond to a child's writing we do the following:

- Child or teacher reads the writing
- We offer some positive feedback
- Teacher often writes some or all of the piece in standard English and offers some teaching points
- Usually we focus on the meaning of the piece first; however, this is affected by the following:
    Confidence and experience of the child.
    Age of the class.
    Time in the year.
    Nature of the activity.
- During the child's time at school equal importance will be given to the development of content and skills. The balance at any one time is effected by the four points above.
- 'Marking' will often mean oral feedback. Written marking which may not always be carried out alongside the child will be written in sentences and will try to encourage a response from the child.

As children become more experienced writers, the length of a particular piece of writing can create problems for the teacher. The length may mean that it is not possible to sit with the child and read the whole piece. Sometimes it is possible to prioritize particular sections of the writing with the intention of covering a different section during each writing conference. At other times it is necessary to take the writing away and respond with written comments. The following vignette is an example of what can be possible when the teacher decides to respond to the writing at a different time.

James had spent the weekly writing workshop over two terms on the writing of a story called 'The Grass Gods'. The final draft was some 20 pages of A4 arranged in 12 short chapters: 1 End of School; 2 The Scrap Piece of Paper; 3 The White Fleshed Emperor; 4 Where do they start?; 5 Giant Corner; 6 The Dark Forest; 7 Died of Fright!; 8 The Poisoned Sword; 9 Magic is in the Air; 10 The Cave; 11 Peter does something good!; 12 Home Sweet Home, but not for long!

The story began like this:

'Class dismissed' said the class teacher after school.
'Hey Thomas' said Peter to his best friend Thomas, 'Thanks for helping me with my maths and for all your set-ups to seal my hat-trick'.
Thomas asked him if he wanted to come to sleep . . .

The teacher decided to read the draft of the story and offer some points for consideration. James was then encouraged to respond in writing to the teacher's points. In this example the child's responses are in italic.

The Grass Gods

Do you need the first part of chapter two? Could the end of chapter one ('maybe he could be that brave . . .') go straight to page three 'NEVER, NEVER, NEVER'?
Yes I think that is a good idea but I would have to change the name of chapter 2 (The Scrap Piece of Paper).

Page 3
Should this be like this? Thomas you have destroyed our land . . . <u>said the strange voice.</u>
Yes I think the spooky voice is good.

Page 6
Where do they get the key from? Do you think this is clear in the story?
No I don't think this is very clear. But they get it on the roof of the door. My new sentence would be . . . It's on the narrow stone on the top of the door.

Page 7
I don't understand 'It's on the top of the roof!'
This means the boy.

Page 8
First the white fleshed emperor helps them then he threatens them. Do you want him to be a friend or an enemy?
This white fleshed emperor is a friend but he wants them to do the mission. He would be cross if they did not do the mission because they were the ones who started the adventure in the first place.

Page 9
Your pictures of the giants are excellent. It works well as you turn the page.

This kind of response to children's writing can provide an informative record of the level of thinking. Detailed responses such as this, and collections of shorter written comments, when accompanied by samples of the child's writing can provide a useful basis for reporting to parents and informing future teachers. This ongoing recording that takes place when responding to children's writing can be more formally structured by developing recording formats.

While thinking about a recording format for the development of writing I was influenced by Smith's (1982) composition/transcription diagram that appears in the PLR handbook. (The PLR is supported by a handbook which offers a theoretical foundation for the use of the record in addition to practical support for the implementation of the record in schools.) My ideas were also influenced by Graves's ideas about recording. During the time when the school was developing its use of the PLR I began to investigate a possible framework for recording observations about children's writing development.

I decided to modify Graves's idea of a writing folder for each child. He outlines how children's writing folders can serve a dual purpose: to organize the children's writing in progress, and for them to be involved in recording their own achievements by filling in labels attached to the folder. For example, Graves suggests that children can be responsible for keeping a record of the

Table 6.1   Observations on writing

Composition	Transcription
'The boy was really happy.' 'This is a poem book.'	9 lines of continuous writing. Kept the same meaning three times when rereading one section.
Decided to complete old book ready for publication in the reading area.	'Random' letter strings. I talked about using greater variety of letters.
'The car was jumping.' Single sheet with picture.	Worked on sound–symbol relationship.
'Q's brother was really mad. These "goras" (white people) came.'	Looked at spelling of brother and word spaces. Used following letters S h o c A e r b a I n.
'Superman, Q's brother is a superman.' Helped C organize writing folder better.	Worked on first letter sound.
'One day the turtle was riding his skateboard.'	More on sounds and letters.
Scary story. Idea from Q. Very good writing.	Very neat letters. Still letter strings, but wider variety.
Checked how scary storybook was going. Wants to read to rest of class.	We decided to make into a big book. I transcribed his meaning, then typed on computer for C to arrange and illustrate.
The car was nearly crashing to the wall.	Long period of help with choosing letters when writing.

transcription skills that they feel confident with. I thought that a label designed for recording children's achievements as writers could be stuck onto the folder. Even if the child was too young to use the label themselves, at least they could be involved by talking to the teacher about their development and seeing the teacher write the record. As often as I could, I made notes about the nature of my interaction with the child, when they were working in the writing area or during a writing workshop. An example of one of the labels is given in Table 6.1.

Table 6.1 comes from a label stuck onto one 6-year-old child's writing folder. It describes some of the individual work done with a child in the class. While reading this, it struck me how much work I had done on sounds and symbols. The work was balanced by some of the more top-down approaches reflected in the composition column. The child concerned had various special needs and proved to be a handful at first. Fortunately he took to the process approach that had been fostered in the classroom. The notes made on the writing folder were made by a variety of adults, including section 11 teachers, bilingual assistants and non-teaching assistants. I sometimes commented on the presentational aspects of the writing, the written form, where the ideas had come from, and how I had helped the child through the process of writing.

I found that keeping the distinction between composition and transcription was hard, and that I began to redefine the areas according to the needs and actions of the children. Often the entries in the composition column would simply represent a translation of a significant part of the writing. This acted as an aide-mémoire and as a demonstration of the quality of the child's language and ideas.

One of the main benefits of an open framework for recording children's progress is the opportunity to record the specific individual characteristics of the young writer's work and development. The amount of structure and detail of any record will have an impact on the opportunity for the teacher to record truly individual characteristics. However, I recognize that some teachers may feel uncomfortable with the open framework that I have illustrated. Appendix I gives an example of a more detailed observation framework that was completed by a student teacher. The PLR was again an influence on the design of the framework.

Developing a recording framework for reading

During the time when the school was developing its language records, we became concerned that the media exaggeration and political speculation concerning reading standards were issues that needed addressing: not in the panic ridden way that was being pushed upon teachers, but through a considered and long-term approach. To complement our observations of children's reading behaviour we decided to design a reading scale which would illustrate our expectations for children at various stages. The 'Becoming a reader' scale outlined in the PLR handbook strongly influenced the school's scale. We wanted to avoid the limitations of the National Curriculum statements of attainment by compiling descriptions of children's natural reading behaviours which as a staff we had all observed regularly. We recognized language development as recursive and holistic, so a simple list of reading skills was not appropriate for our needs. In addition, the distinctive needs of the bilingual children in the school, which the staff had learnt to identify, were not part of other diagrams which attempted to map reading progress.

We felt that the crucial stage where children move from using memory and picture cues into one-to-one correspondence needed to be clear. This proved to be a particularly difficult step for some pupils, and at times was frustrating for the teachers, who were facing pressure to conform to national norms. We also wanted to acknowledge the book handling skills that children developed in the nursery. Many of the children entering the nursery had had limited experience of the kind of picture fiction that was being offered. However, they quickly developed their understanding about the reading process and we were keen that this should be recognized and affirmed.

Having established the scale, we had a tool for monitoring children's progress in reading throughout the school over a period of time. At this time the 'standards' debate on reading was at a new peak. Martin Turner's views had been seized upon by the media, and schools were coming under pressure to prove their success in teaching reading, typically through standardized reading tests. Although I felt an overview of the reading achievements was important, I was determined not to succumb to simplistic, dated and culturally biased testing procedures. As a school we felt that the expertise of the staff should be used to structure the kind of framework that we chose to adopt. The scale the school produced enabled us to reflect on how children were progressing from year to year. Not surprisingly, this process raised as many questions as it answered.

During the third term of the academic year 1990/1991 all staff assessed their children using the reading scale; this was repeated for 1991/1992, again in the third term. Figure 6.2 shows the levels which the year two children achieved. The left bar of each pair represents 90/91 and the right bar 91/92. The chart shows that more children were achieving higher levels in 91/92; noticeably, there were fewer children in the 'tackling print' stage. These seemed to have been distributed in the 'non-fluent' and 'fluent' categories particularly. This seemed to be positive; however, the important question was what were the reasons for the changes. If the results of the data were to positively affect policy decisions, we had to speculate on what had brought them about.

Prior to the 91/92 results the school had embarked on an intensive period of whole school language development and INSET. It was felt that this initiative probably contributed to the improved results. Having only established data collection for two years it was not possible to see long-term trends. We also had to take into account the possibility that the chart could simply represent a difference in the abilities of the children in that particular year. As language coordinator I also felt we needed more work on agreeing what constituted achievement of a particular stage, despite my confidence that because of much shared practice, staff would record accurate results. However, the process we went through in developing the scale was important in developing our professional understanding of how children learn to read, in addition to providing us with a tool for monitoring that reading behaviour.

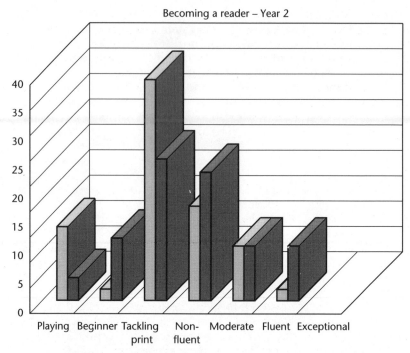

Figure 6.2 Comparison of reading levels

The reading scale gave us a quick overview and was used in conjunction with the more detailed observational framework for children's reading behaviour. In the white Observation and Samples section of the PLR, section 3 gives an excellent framework for recording observations of children's reading; the idea being that the samples are collated to give information for summative comments which are written on the main form. As the school was not adopting the complete record, we felt it would be useful to adapt the 'Reading Sample' format for our own reading observations which were carried out in the first and third terms of the academic year. Figure 6.3 shows the original on the left and our format on the right.

Overall the staff wanted a simpler format which related to the school's particular circumstances. We had decided that the reading sample would usually be informal assessment, with running record and miscue analysis being used only occasionally for children whose behaviour was particularly complex; hence the 'sampling procedure' was omitted. We wanted to include the 'child's own perception' of her/his reading progress, as we were not using the formal document which addresses this perspective. The 'strategies' section was very similar; however, I felt that the child's 'previous experience' was not evident from reading aloud and was very difficult to evaluate. Additionally, the children at the school used their 'memory' of known stories extensively, and we felt there might be some connection with the rote learning of the Koran, so we added this extra strategy.

Each section of the PLR in some way contributed to the way we chose to

Figure 6.3   Modifications to PLR reading sample

Title of book/text (fiction or information)

Known/unknown text

Sampling procedure used:
informal assessment/running record/ miscue analysis

Overall impression of the child's reading:
• confidence and degree of independence
• involvement in the book/text
• the way in which the child read the text aloud

Strategies the child used when reading aloud:
• drawing on previous experience to make sense of the book/text
• playing at reading
• using book language
• reading the pictures
• focusing on print (directionality, 1:1 correspondence, recognition of certain words)
• using semantic/syntactic/graphophonic cues
• predicting
• self correcting
• using several strategies or over-dependent on one

Child's response to the book/text:
• personal response
• critical response (understanding, evaluating, appreciating wider meanings)

What this sample shows about the child's development as a reader

Experiences/support needed to further development

Overview
• Range
• Independence
• Motivation

Child's own perception

Strategies used while reading alone or sharing a book
• playing at reading
• using book language
• reading the pictures
• memory
• focusing on print
• balance of semantic, syntactic, graphophonic cues
• self correction

Views of text
• Personal – e.g. relate to own experience
• Critical/analytical – appreciate wider meanings/issues

---

record language achievements across the school. The formal document influenced the structure of our home visits; the observation and samples framework and the handbook contributed to the teaching and learning of reading and writing in the school. Having the power to tailor the format to our own requirements was a very important process in the school's language policy work, and contrasted with the inflexible demands of national assessment requirements.

One of the innovative features of the PLR was the distinction between the semi-structured observations frameworks and the summative document. Both of these formats allow for the teacher's written observations of the children in their class. In the following section I describe how one school approached the observation framework through the use of reading diaries. One of the interesting aspects of these diaries was the way that parents' comments, pupil's book reviews and the teacher's observations were written in the same book. This enabled the teachers to build up a relatively rich picture of the child's development as a reader.

Recording reading: another school's approach

The final section of this chapter looks at the work of a school that decided to unify teacher comments, parent comments and pupil book reviews within the reading diaries that each pupil was given. The advantage of this system was that all interested parties were able to see a rich, developing picture of the child's development as a reader. The teachers were able to use this information for any summative records such as annual report writing.

In the early years classes, the reading diaries accompanied any books that were sent home with the child. When the parents had shared a book with their child they were encouraged to comment or sign the diary to confirm that the child had read their book. Here are some examples of parents' comments:

> I agree she uses the pictures to help sometimes. We think she did very well. Thankyou.
> I am still trying to get Jeremy to follow the book rather than memorize.
> Karen was not interested in reading the book. I kept trying with her but she just wouldn't do it. I don't know if it is because she's at home.
> Lewis read well the words previously learned – Rosie/saw etc. Still to learn the number words one, two etc. as he counted the objects.
> There are quite a few new words in this book which Jean is struggling with. She still prefers to guess words rather than spell them.

The comments that the parents made gave the teacher an indication of their thinking about how their child was learning to read. If the parent had any misconceptions and/or anxieties about the reading process, the teachers were able to inform the parents based on their experience with greater numbers of children. The teachers were also able to show the parents that some of the child's strategies that might have appeared to be negative were actually positive indications of a developing reader. The tightly structured use of a variety of reading scheme materials was evident from comments about the learning of new words. The controlled vocabulary and gradual introduction of new words was quite different from the notion that children often learn to read by repetitive experiences with a core of favourite books.

As the children became more experienced readers, they were encouraged to

Figure 6.4   Book review format from reading diary

Book title: Author/level:
Date started:
Date finished:

What was the book about?

Which part did you enjoy the most?

Who was your favourite character? Why?

What did you learn?

Was the book easy, medium, or hard?

Give the book a mark out of 10.

What Katy Did
Susan M Coolidge

Started 23 Nov 1993
Finished 31 Jan 1994

The book is about a girl called Katy who was the oldest of six. She was a tomboy. One day she was playing on a swing and the rope broke. She fell off and when she woke up she couldn't move her legs. It takes four years for her to get better. I liked the part where it told you about a place they called paradise, the children would go there for picnics. My favourite character was cousin Helen because she is like a teacher and she is also very kind. I learnt if you are happy you can get better a lot quicker. The book was medium. I would give it 9/10.

---

complete reviews for some of the books that they had read. They were given a framework to help them structure the writing (Figure 6.4).

After two years of using the reading diaries the headteacher asked for a review of progress. The review was to consider how well the diaries were being used and what could be learned about the school's language and literacy development. The language coordinator collected six reading diaries from each teacher. From these diaries she transferred extracts of interest onto computer. One of the reasons for this was so that all colleagues would have the opportunity to see how the diaries progressed throughout the school. Alongside the extracts the coordinator raised issues that she felt were important as far as the school's language policy was concerned.

An INSET meeting was held where all staff read the snapshot of reading diary extracts. This had become quite a substantial document, as it contained extracts from 36 diaries. The purpose of the meeting was to decide on future developments for the diaries and for the teaching and learning of language and literacy. The recorded comments of teachers, parents and children were helping the staff to improve the curriculum and pedagogy. To give an example of the kinds of comment that were recorded, I have included a small number of them in Table 6.2.

One of the underlying reasons for the review was the hope that the process of the review itself would stimulate discussions and action on better continuity

Table 6.2 Snapshot from reading diary review document

Name of child	Title of book read to teacher	Teacher's comments in reading diaries	Parents' comments in reading diaries	Children's book reviews	Language coordinator's comments concerning the reading diary entries
James	Not So Silly Billy	Find out where the stick insects were hiding. On her h---. On a p---.	Pages 11–24 James read amazingly well!		Janice [the teacher] set up an activity in the diary to develop word recognition based on some of the words in the child's text. I learned later on that James also set up games for the teacher.
Tim	A Jar of Crystals	Tim, if you need to sound words out, try to sound more than one letter at a time, you might find it easier.		The book was about green crystals. I enjoyed the bit where Bridget and Peter found the jar of crystals. My favourite character was Peter. I enjoyed the book because it was scary. Peter was my favourite character because he was funny. The book was easy.10/10	If children of this age are capable of this kind of review, do the more experienced children require a more searching format?
Martin	Diary of a Honey Bee	T. Write down one interesting fact about bees. C. Every day a worker bee makes about enough honey to cover a pin. T. That's interesting; no wonder we need such a lot of bees.			This is similar to the idea of response journals where the teacher develops a written dialogue.
Dheerna	The New Bike	I still feel Dheerna has struggled with this book She has read it to me but has had lots of support in some basic words. I will change this book as I don't want to get 'stuck' in one place. She is cooperating quite well and is keen to read. This is a great improvement.	I thought Dheerna read quite well.		At this stage some of the children are being asked to comment on the book orally using the reading diary format. Does this happen in reception?

throughout the school. The language coordinator's comments were added to the review document to focus people's minds on the appropriate issues and to quicken the development of continuity in a non-confrontational way.

There was some variation in the number of comments that were made by teachers and in the depth of those comments. A minimum number of written comments for each child per year was agreed. It was felt that this straight-forward target would help everyone feel confident that they had recorded enough information. The quality and depth of the comments was an issue that was partly related to professional development. One of the teachers commented that sometimes it was difficult to find the right words. The snapshot of comments from the reading diaries was a help in this respect, and it was decided to include it as an appendix of the policy document.

Many of the teachers' comments were related to the use of reading scheme texts. During the previous period of policy work it had been agreed to supplement the structure of the reading scheme with a wide range of other texts that were displayed in the reading area. It followed that if these other texts were being used effectively, the teachers' comments in the reading diaries should at times reflect the use of these texts during reading conference. The implication was that when teachers were sharing books with children or 'hearing them read', the other books in the classroom would have to be part of that interaction.

Observations on higher order reading skills were rare in comparison with observations on other reading behaviour. It was recognized by the staff that these were difficult to categorize and tended to be evident in various tasks throughout the day. It was felt that some work needed to be done in clarifying what some of the skills and issues were in relation to higher order reading. Following this period of clarification, decisions could be made on how children could be further supported.

Most of the observations from teachers, parents and children were based on the reading of fiction. Although a much wider range of reading was going on, it was not being recorded in the reading diaries. It was felt that fiction was a particularly important form for children and was one that they regularly chose. However, the importance of reading a range of texts was also recognized. This raised a number of implications for classroom organization of texts and reading times.

The diaries were producing a wealth of information about the children in the school. It was clear from the parents' comments that more work needed to be done on explaining how the school approached reading, and particularly the developmental characteristics of learning to read. The school had organized a literacy week, during which there was an information evening for parents that was very well attended. It was decided to produce an information sheet for parents to supplement the range of information on reading that the school provided that was published by other organizations.

In this chapter I have looked at the merits of a naturalistic system that encourages teachers to record their observations of children's language and literacy learning. The philosophies and style of the PLR make this an important model for recording achievements. One of the implications of using such formats is that teachers and coordinators need time to read and reflect on the kinds of comment they make if they are to improve children's learning and their own professional development.

SEVEN

The links with reading

The holistic nature of language and literacy means that the approach that the teacher adopts for writing will have implications for reading and talking. In many teachers' minds there is a significant link between reading and writing, and this is reinforced by a classroom emphasis on these two modes. The process approach to writing has close links with the 'real book approach' to reading. This chapter outlines a current description of the real book approach in practice; it then shows the links with the process approach. The final part of the chapter identifies some theoretical and research findings which are used to reflect on how the real book approach has continued to develop. Reflections on the development of the real book approach point to some issues for the use of the process approach.

Much has been written in recent years about the real book approach. Some of this writing has appeared in the national media and unfortunately the views expressed have often been ill-informed ones. Other writers have tended to assume that the real book approach has remained static and chained to a number of influential authors who were writing in the '70s and '80s. The criticisms of the real book approach have focused on three main issues: the real book approach does not involve any teaching and encourages the children to learn on their own; standards of reading are lower when the approach is used; and phonics are not taught.

In the following section I outline what the real book approach consists of in practice. In the course of this discussion I hope to illustrate that the first point above is simplistic and wrong. The issue of standards is a complex one, and I do not intend to cover it in detail here, as other authors have provided an examination of this area (e.g. Wray 1994). However, I will refer briefly to a study that attempted to look at the differing standards achieved by the real book approach compared to formal teaching methods. As far as the third point above is concerned, the real book approach does not preclude the teaching of phonics. Phonics is taught according to the needs of the individual children in the class. The teaching of phonics is balanced with the teaching of the other cueing strategies that the children need in order to be effective and motivated readers. I do not intend to cover this complex issue in great depth; however, I refer to the issue of phonics in the theory section of this chapter.

The real book approach

The real book approach is a demanding but potentially exciting approach to reading. Teachers who use the approach recognize that the teaching and learning of reading is a complex process. One of the implications of using the approach is that in order to be an effective teacher of reading you need a view outside your own classroom. This view is found through reading about the work of other teachers' and other educationists' experiences of the teaching of reading. The best results are achieved by combining classroom experience, research findings, theoretical opinions and the consensus of other knowledgeable teachers. As Liz Waterland pointed out:

> Classroom practice should always have a firm and respectable intellectual basis. We cannot any longer – if we ever really could – offer only feelings or instincts or experience as our rationale. This is especially true if we are changing established practice. What will be our justification? Is what we are planning better only in our opinion or can we find support from outside authorities? Any change should deepen and enlarge our understanding of children, reading and teaching.
>
> (Waterland 1985: 7)

The fundamental theory underlying the real book approach is the child's control over their learning. First and foremost this is reflected in their opportunity to choose the text that they are reading; this choice directly affects their motivation to read. The notion of choice is often absent or minimal during the exclusive use of a reading scheme where the books that are read are decided by the teacher, who is guided by the hierarchy of the scheme. This point does require some qualification: some of the most recent changes to major reading schemes have included the introduction of choice within a particular reading level. Additionally, many teachers combine the use of real books with the use of a reading scheme or a variety of schemes, and this combines some choice with the limits of the scheme. (It is interesting to note that reading schemes are rarely used in their entirety or strictly according to the publishers' recommendations.)

Some children will enter the nursery or reception class able to read. Their parents will have offered them a rich diet of reading materials, and their positive interaction will have helped the child develop quickly. These children will have developed strong preferences about their reading materials and will be able to make effective choices about what they read. It seems to be a backward step to force these children to progress through a reading scheme. Provided such children are regularly assessed, there is no reason why they cannot continue to develop as fluent and motivated readers who choose their own texts.

Offering children maximum control over their reading materials does not mean that the teacher does nothing to guide that choice. Some children choose texts that are inappropriate for them: the teacher offers support and guidance, which includes emphasizing the importance of understanding the meaning of what is being read. The teacher also offers strategies for choosing a book: 'Have you tried "Red Letter Day"?'; 'Share "Willy the Wimp" with Rachel to see if you like it'; 'Ask Rabinda to recommend something'; 'Read the back cover to see if you might like the book'; 'Read the first page to check it's not too hard'; 'Why not try another Gene Kemp book'; 'Try skimming through that information book' etc.

At times children choose texts that are too difficult to read. This is not always negative, as they can be learning through discussion about the pictures, and through fragments of text that they do understand. Occasionally the realization that a text is too hard can act as a motivation to improve reading ability, which is why Key Stage 1 classrooms should contain a small number of books that are particularly demanding, such as longer children's novels. However, if a child consistently chooses texts that are too difficult, they are offered the necessary level of guidance on choosing appropriate texts. In some cases the teacher may request that the child reads a recommended book or books. In these cases the teacher is always looking to give control back to the child when they think the child can make sensible choices.

The teacher can also use the classroom organization to structure reading. This is how one teacher describes part of her classroom organization:

> At first the children seemed reluctant to make real choices. I had to encourage them to bring books from home. The children mainly brought story books. I decided to introduce a day when I wanted them to bring in different kinds of texts. I found that they brought football magazines and programmes, magazines for young people, facts books, personal organizers etc. I also introduced a weekly poetry session which was very popular. The atmosphere in the classroom was quite different on these days. The children tended to collaborate much more and talk about the texts. I also felt that I still wanted children's novels to be an important part of their reading so I often recommended that a child should try a story book having read a series of non-fiction books.

The physical organization of reading materials is seen to be a particularly important part of the real book approach. The reading area of the classroom is often a comfortable, carpeted area with the books attractively displayed, some with front covers visible. The wall displays often have posters and information to do with reading, and the area can be enhanced by using plants and table top displays, for example a display of books for 'author of the week'. Having organized the physical space, the teacher has the important job of deciding the kinds of text that are present. The importance of the texts themselves cannot be over-emphasized; this is one of the most significant aspects of the real book approach. The choice of fiction depends on the teacher's developing knowledge of the books themselves. With picture fiction this is a quicker process because the teacher reads more of them on a daily basis and they are shorter. Longer children's novels are more of a problem due to the amount of time they take to read. However, there are publications that offer reviews of books, and it is necessary to take advice from knowledgeable booksellers, librarians, local authority services, other teachers etc. while the teacher's knowledge of longer texts develops. The range of texts that children read, again hinges on the classroom organization. Non-fiction can be built up as the children research particular areas of interest to them throughout the year. Cross-curricular topics also present opportunities to gather collections of non-fiction. Environmental print is tackled through specific activities and displays, as is work on media; some schools have newspapers delivered that are available for regular use.

Daily reading times are necessary to maintain the real book approach. All children in the class are encouraged to read books that they have chosen for, say, 20 to 30 minutes. This gives the teacher the opportunity to work closely with children and to explore many of the issues to do with reading that may arise. Other classroom activities will also involve the development of reading, but the reading time gives the teacher a clear focus on reading as a discrete part of the language curriculum. This time might include small group work and pairs work when appropriate.

The style of teacher–pupil interaction during reading time is shaped by the reading conference. The implication behind this term is that the interaction is more collaborative in nature, with the progress of the conference being negotiated by both the teacher and the child. This is not to say that direct intervention by the teacher is precluded, but there is a negotiated balance – based on the needs of the child – that ensures that the child is offered the kind of interaction that is appropriate. For some children this may consist of a discussion about their views of a text: 'How did that Roald Dahl book compare with *The Borrowers* which you read a few weeks ago?' For others the interaction may be focused much more on their understanding of the specific passage that they are reading: 'What has happened to the ice baby?' For still others the phonetic cueing strategies may receive teaching: 'You've got the first two letters, what sound do the letters "ing" make?' The teacher is able to be more flexible and responsive to the child's needs which become evident when reading aloud or sharing a book with the teacher.

In contrast with some reading schemes it was quite common for the teacher to listen to children read while a range of other activities was going on. The nature of their interaction was significantly different. The controlled vocabulary of the schemes and an emphasis on phonetics resulted in the teacher acting mainly as someone who checked the child's ability to decode. Often this resulted in the teacher correcting the child too quickly, or supplying words that the child was unsure about, without encouraging the child to use a range of decoding strategies.

The teacher reading aloud to the whole class is a daily occurrence. The class reader has an important place to play in this, as it enables the teacher to share texts with the children that they may not have thought to choose. Some Local Education Authority book services offer sets of the same title for children to follow and discuss. Reading aloud enables the teacher to open discussions that are relevant to the text in question. These discussions range from questions asked by the children, to the teacher's own teaching and learning points, including opportunities to assess the children's depth of understanding. With younger children, many more picture books are read at each reading aloud session. Some of the picture fiction will be read over and over again, as this enables the children to become more and more familiar with the text. It also mirrors the behaviour evident in the bedtime reading cycle (Holdaway 1979). In addition to the regular reading of fiction, a range of other texts is used. Relevant newspaper stories can be discussed; regular prepared poetry reading takes place; children sharing work in progress and finished books, puppet shows, scripted drama, and the reading of non-fiction all extend the range of texts that the children experience.

The parents' role is seen to be very important for the real book approach, and effective school policies on home–school reading partnerships are vital. The best schemes encourage the parents to take an active role in their child's reading. Often this is supported by the use of reading diaries which are used for the parents to comment on the child's reading (see Chapter 6 for an example of the use of reading diaries). If the teacher's comments are included in these diaries, the teacher can model the kind of language and issues that the parents may need to be aware of. Sometimes these reading diaries can evolve into a constructive dialogue between parent and teacher where both parties learn more about the development of reading and the child's place in that development. The learning at school should flow into the home and vice versa, with the child bringing texts from home if they want to.

There is often a minority of children who make poor choices of reading material, and in these cases it is sometimes appropriate to use a reading scheme in order to structure more carefully the kinds of text they read. Ideally the teacher should decide on a sequence of real books for the child to read, but sometimes the constraints of time make this difficult to achieve. Additionally, if it is observed that the child's phonetic cueing and concept of word are limited, the controlled vocabulary of the scheme may provide suitable texts. For the teacher, the difficulty is weighing up the potential demotivation that the scheme may engender against the possible benefits of an emphasis on phonetics, decoding and structure.

Any approach to the teaching and learning of reading will probably result in some children who struggle to read. The important thing is that those children are spotted early and that practical steps are taken to support them. Among the options available to the teacher is the opportunity to try a different approach or strategy. There will be children for whom a diet of reading scheme(s) and phonics simply has not worked. Teachers must have the knowledge and confidence to remove the child from the scheme and suggest a series of suitable texts for the child. Additionally, careful evaluations need to be made of exactly what the child's needs seem to be. Marie Clay (1989) suggested that 'reading recovery' consists of taking a holistic approach to language development, diagnosing where the child's weaknesses are and offering support in those areas. This implies a genuine understanding of a range of strategies and approaches that are matched with the child's difficulties. Too often, a narrow diet of phonics that may have contributed to reading difficulties is reinforced by yet more phonics. This is not taking a balanced approach. A special needs coordinator reflected on such a child:

> Darren had struggled with his reading throughout the school. I asked if I could read with him one day. It was an uncomfortable experience. His

intonation and expression was very low. He stopped and stared when he didn't know a word. If he was stuck on a word he would sound out every letter. The result of this often didn't give him enough of a clue to the word because he wasn't using the other cueing strategies to support his reading. When I asked him about sections that he had read he would only offer minimal information. The class teacher felt that I should give him more phonics practice and that perhaps we should try earlier books in the reading scheme. My heart sank because I knew that the boy had had phonics and reading schemes throughout the school. Knowing that my daughter had learnt to read by the time she was three simply by sharing and discussing books and other texts, I wondered whether a variation on this would work with Darren.

Detailed and regular recording is another important feature of the real book approach. The recording process should enable the teacher to assess the child's development as a reader and decide on future action to support the child. Chapter 6 covers recording in more detail and includes examples of the process of recording reading and writing.

Some links between real books and the process approach

I have briefly described the main practical elements of the real book approach. If we think about these in relation to the process approach there are a number of similarities. Table 7.1 illustrates some of the links between the real book and process approaches.

The child's control over their own learning is central to both approaches. This is based on the assumption that the child is an active learner who is capable of making some decisions for themselves. It is also recognized that motivation is a fundamental concern during the teaching and learning process. When students are given control over their learning, their enthusiasm

Table 7.1 Comparison of real book approach with process approach

Real book approach	Process approach to writing
• Child choice over text to read	• Child choice over text to write
• Reading/listening areas in classroom	• Writing/role-play areas
• Daily whole class reading time	• Regular writing workshop
• Emphasis on real books	• Emphasis on children's own writing
• Daily sharing of books/texts	• Sharing of drafts and finished writing
• Reading conferences	• Writing conferences
• School/home partnerships	• Writing at home brought to school. Writing at school taken home to chosen audience
• Collaborative /shared reading	• Collaborative writing
• Holistic reading recovery methods	
• Naturalistic recording methods	• Naturalistic recording methods

is tapped into, resulting in more commitment to the particular concept, skill or area of knowledge.

The creation of language and literacy areas in the classroom is common to both approaches. The reading area should be a standard feature of any classroom. This area is supported by other collections of books where necessary, such as themed book displays, non-fiction collections, learning resources (dictionaries, atlases etc.). The writing area can work well with younger children; a range of resources is organized to stimulate the children to engage in a variety of writing styles. Role-play areas are also useful to stimulate natural literate behaviour. For example, phones and message pads along with other office resources can provide the starting point for a work environment that encourages the children to take on new roles. For older children, writing tends to be covered by the writing workshop and as a medium of more general learning through the teacher's planned tasks. The increasing abstraction of the work means that specific curriculum area bays become less practical; however, resources are grouped together and clearly labelled to encourage the children's independence.

Contrary to the perception that both approaches are informal, they rely on a significant degree of whole class activities. This gives the teacher the opportunity to focus specifically on reading or writing. The whole class organization can support the teacher in specifically focusing on the more complex issues surrounding language and literacy. It also helps to create a particular atmosphere conducive to the understanding of a shared enterprise.

With the real book approach the teacher and the class take control over text selection. This enables the teacher to supply a range of books that are relevant to the children they are teaching. This is in contrast to the reading scheme, where the writers and publishers control the texts that are part of the package. With the process approach to writing the children also have initial and direct control over the texts they write. This contrasts with set activities where the teacher controls the nature of the writing expected as an outcome of the task.

Both approaches encourage a flexible approach to the sharing of texts. The sharing of texts with the whole class is important in a number of ways. The sharing time provides models of complete texts and extracts. With reading, the children hear a wider range of texts and are encouraged to think about these texts in a way they might not were they reading alone. With writing, the initial drafts provide inspiration for other children in the class. The reading of books that the children have written and published gives the author the opportunity to test the peer group's response to the text.

Literacy conferences are the time when the teacher's interaction skills are most important. The teacher is able to assess progress and offer suggestions for the ways forward. The style of the conference is one where the teacher is acutely aware of the difference in power between herself and the pupil. The teacher learns from the child how best to help them and, over time, how best to help all the children they teach. During the interaction the teacher hopes to offer the child as much independence and ability to solve their own problems as the child can manage.

A significant realization arising from the research over the last 20 years that has looked at language and literacy is the vital importance of strong home/school links. With reading, this needs to include the gradual re-education of some parents with regard to the things they do with their children that help the children's reading. This is not to deny that parents offer much instinctively good teaching to their children, but it is in recognition of the teachers' experience of many children over the years and the wider picture accessed through published accounts. With writing, the hope is that primary children of all ages will write for pleasure at home and bring that writing to continue or share during the writing workshop. Another good indicator of a high level of motivation is when children choose to continue work at home that they have started at school. A two-way channel of teaching and learning between home and school, parent and teacher, begins to open up.

The real book approach has undergone significant changes through teachers' continuing experience with the practice and theory. Because of the theoretical links between the process approach to writing and the real book approach to reading, there are a number of similarities in the practice. In the next section I examine the development of the theory of real books. Finally, by reflecting on developments in the practice and theory of reading, I suggest some future directions for the process approach to writing.

Theory and research

During the 1980s a core of influential authors were advocating an approach to reading that emphasized the place of real books as opposed to reading scheme books. These authors felt that children were not empty vessels to be filled with knowledge and skills, but that they were active learners who were capable of taking responsibility for significant aspects of their development. Meek (1988) argued for the vital importance of the particular texts that teachers offer children and the ways these texts help children to learn. She clearly set out a number of important reasons why real books had many advantages over reading scheme books. Waterland (1985) offered a school and classroom context for the teaching of reading using real books. Frank Smith's work became internationally famous (or infamous). His readable style contained provocative thoughts on the teaching and learning of literacy, including his ideas on 'the fallacy of phonics' (Smith 1978: 50). He believed that learning to talk was closely linked with learning to read and write. He suggested that children should be encouraged to join 'the literacy club' in order to become readers and writers. The literacy club was seen as the community of language and literacy users who supported children in their understanding of reading and writing. Smith felt that the way that we learn to talk offered important pointers to the ways we might learn to read and write.

Perhaps the most respected of all the real book theorists was Kenneth Goodman. His most important contribution was the greater awareness he generated in terms of the reading cues – semantic, syntactic and graphophonic – through his work on miscue analysis. Memorably he called reading a 'psycholinguistic guessing game'.

These authors have come under close scrutiny; Roger Beard's book *Teaching Literacy Balancing Perspectives* contains a series of chapters that attack the theoretical basis to much of Smith and Goodman's work. Reid (1993) is one of the contributors who makes such an attack. In portraying their theories she offers a view of the real book approach that perhaps is extreme. One of her opinions is that no 'teaching' is involved in the real book approach. Common to other contributors in the book, Reid suggests that the views of Smith and Goodman 'have been extremely influential' (Reid 1993: 23).

Much of the criticism of real books and whole language approaches is based on the view that these approaches have had a wide ranging and negative influence on a large number of teachers. I believe this view reveals a significant flaw in the argument put forward by some of the 'new phonics' adherents (Adams 1990). My own experience of primary teachers is that very few have adopted the theories and practices of real book advocates. In addition, my contacts with the advisory services of four authorities have offered the same evidence. This anecdotal evidence can be backed up by research evidence which shows that teachers who use the real book approach are very much in a minority. If this is the case, there are serious implications for the debate on standards of reading and teaching methods. If the case can be proved that standards in reading are falling, and if a causal link is to be drawn between lower standards and reading pedagogy, perhaps attention should be turned to the true amount, quality and nature of phonics instruction that is currently taking place in British primary schools.

The research evidence is strong that real book philosophies are practised only in a very small number of schools. In a survey of 110 randomly selected schools in Northern Ireland, Gray (1983: 30) revealed that 'a large rural school was the only school in the sample in which beginners were taught to read through the use of *Breakthrough* materials alone'. It is possible that there were schools who used the real book approach and that the questionnaire did not allow them to record this evidence; however, I think this is unlikely. Assuming that the language experience approach represented by *Breakthrough* was the closest that schools got to the real book approach, this study provides clear evidence of the extent of the real book approach.

Rice (1987) surveyed all the primary schools in 'a large northern industrial city'. One hundred and ninety six of the 199 schools returned the questionnaire, and only two of the schools claimed *not* to use a reading scheme. Once again, if it is accepted that the use of a reading scheme implies that the schools were not following the real book approach, the number of schools is very small.

Similar evidence of minimal use of the real book approach was recorded by Cato *et al.* (1992). Their study was titled *The Teaching of Initial Literacy: How do Teachers do it?*, and consisted of 234 randomly selected schools across England and Wales. One hundred and twenty two headteachers completed a questionnaire that asked for information on the range of methods used by Year 2 teachers. A smaller sub-section of schools were visited to add to the data provided by the questionnaires. On the teaching of reading the authors commented that:

> In view of the recurrent debate about the use of 'real books', it must first of all be pointed out that only four percent of headteachers taking part

in the survey claimed their schools exclusively used 'real books' in teaching reading. This replicates the findings of Her Majesty's Inspectorate (DES 1990).

(Cato *et al.* 1992: 22)

The second problem that some of the new phonics theorists have is their concentration on authors like Smith and Goodman who were at the height of their popularity in the '70s and '80s. Since then both the theory and the practice of real books have moved forward. Teachers have refined the practice, and this has been shared with researchers and writers, who have come to new understandings.

Campbell (1992) felt that the real book approach has four crucial elements: the books; the child; the teacher; and the interaction centred on a book, which brings together the learner and the teacher. Of course, these elements apply to any approach to reading. The significant difference is that with the real book approach the teacher and the children retain more control over these elements. The sequence of books is not necessarily prescribed, the language is not restricted, and the interaction is less inflexible. The emphasis on a reading scheme removes the teacher's control over the kind of text, and can affect the nature of interaction by encouraging the teacher to indiscriminately focus on decoding and phonetic cueing. A greater level of control enables the teacher to address the child's immediate needs in a flexible and appropriate way. The idea that the real book approach is a 'non-teaching' one is refuted by Campbell.

In early shared reading the teacher might read the story to the child and encourage the child to retell the story, support the child in his/her attempt to read on his/her own or enable the child to read alongside the teacher. In such an apprenticeship approach (Waterland 1988) the role of the teacher and of the child will be constantly evolving. Subsequently, the teacher will listen to the child read, compare that reading to the text, making judgements as to the amount of support the child requires, and then provide the support or teaching which helps the child immediately and perhaps suggests strategies for the future.

(Campbell 1992: 3)

The kinds of method and strategy outlined earlier in this chapter also form much of Burman's (1990) view of the real book approach. The teacher's role is again shown to be one of importance, and with a much wider range of activities than the traditional role. The direct teaching that goes on is often set within a wider context. For example, the teacher may take on the role of a customer in the class role-play area:

T: Good morning, I'd like an apple and a bag of salt and vinegar crisps please.
C: I haven't got any apples.
T: I wonder what I could have instead?
C: I've got some oranges.
T: Good. I'll have an orange and a bag of salt and vinegar crisps please.

[Child is unsure of the correct bag to choose]
T: It begins with an S.
C: Fifty pence please.
T: Could you make me a list of the things you sell in your shop? I will come and pick it up in ten minutes.
C: Bye.

In this example the teacher directs the dialogue towards her goal of encouraging the child to write a list. The dialogue becomes an opportunity for writing, and subsequently the reading of the list of foods that the shop sells. During the role-play the teacher is able to develop the decoding skills of the child by referring to the letter S. The experience connects the language modes (and other curriculum areas) through a context that is more meaningful for the child. The teaching of reading in this example has not involved the correction of the child's reading errors or the use of flash cards to test the child's knowledge of words, but it did involve effective teaching.

Surprisingly, research evidence that compares the relative merits of the real book approach compared with the use of reading schemes is rare, yet it is the kind of question that taxes many teachers. In part this is because it is extremely difficult to provide the kind of concrete cause and effect findings that teachers may want. However, Bridge (1990) describes just such a project. The study compared two school populations of 5-year-old pupils. Qualitative research methods included logs that the teachers kept throughout the year, structured interviews with the teachers at the end of the year, and structured interviews with pupils at the beginning and end of the year. A quantitative element was provided by the Burt graded reading test. The data was gathered for two years. The two schools were part of a local authority project and there is no indication whether both schools were as efficient as each other in the use of their chosen approaches. One school took a 'traditional' approach and the other a 'whole language approach' that included the use of real books.

The findings indicated that the whole language pupils seemed to be slow to 'take off'. However, in the long term the whole language group gained advantage through a number of factors:

- more positive attitude shown in
  - greater membership of public libraries;
  - greater voluntary use of books;
  - more positive self image as readers;
- superior storying abilities
- greater use of expression when reading aloud
- wider use of positive reading cues and strategies
- negligible use of inappropriate or negative reading cues and strategies

(Bridge 1990: 178)

Wray (1994) suggested that the ways forward in the teaching and learning of reading are to be found by using research results and opinion from both sides of the debate. The interactive model of reading implies that bottom-up approaches that concentrate on letters, sounds and words should be coupled with top-down approaches that emphasize genuine purposes and contexts.

These contexts give children the experience of learning about whole texts as opposed to decontextualized drills. This synthesis of approaches is also outlined by Harrison (1992), who makes the important point that the needs of the reader are such that the emphasis required on word recognition or comprehension is constantly variable. The implications for the teacher are that their teaching must reflect the fact that not all children will require the same kind of support or the same approach.

Future directions – from reading to writing

The small minority of schools who have remained committed to the teaching and learning of reading with real books have evaluated and developed the theories and practices that were prevalent in the '70s and '80s. These developments offer a more realistic and potentially exciting direction for future work by teachers. The links between the theories of the real book approach and the process approach to writing enable us to compare the possible future directions for both approaches.

The current practice of the real book approach offers some interesting issues for future development; the following list illustrates some of these:

- The level of control that children are offered should be appropriate to the individual.
- Reading schemes will offer possibilities for some children.
- Choice can be organized to provide a simpler structure for some children.
- A direct focus on phonetics and interaction to support phonetic understanding will sometimes be necessary.
- Children who are struggling must be identified early and given more support.
- Some children need to be directed to read particular texts.
- An emphasis on semantics is offered to children who offer nonsense substitutions and who repeatedly try unsuccessfully to sound words out.
- An emphasis on phonetics and whole words is offered to children who consistently use memory and picture cues too much.
- Teachers' strategies when hearing children read should be part of a continuum between an emphasis on learning to read, and critical discussions on reading and texts. They are dependent on the individual child and the context.
- Higher order reading is actively developed, particularly through the teacher's expert choice of texts and their knowledge of the issues such texts generate.
- The ability to make appropriate choices is explicitly developed.
- The complexities of how people learn to read are explored with the children.

Some of the implications for future reading practice outlined so far have implications for the teaching of writing. This is in part because of the relationship between reading and writing. If we take the bullet points above, some can be directly related and some indirectly related to the teaching of writing.

- The level of control that children are offered should be appropriate to the individual.

During writing workshop and work in the writing area, most children will be able to successfully generate appropriate ideas for their writing. However, the teacher will intervene where necessary to give children ideas for their writing. This complements the writing tasks that are offered at other times. The teacher may plan an individual series of writing workshop activities for a child. These would be inspired by the work of other children in the class and the particular child's interests. The teacher would also draw on their developing experience of writing workshop to provide suggestions that would motivate the child.

- A direct focus on phonetics and interaction to support phonetic understanding will sometimes be necessary.

Direct focus on secretarial aspects of the writing process will sometimes be necessary. Spelling will need regular attention with many children. On the whole this work is done with the individual child, because the written draft provides a meaningful context for such teaching. However, the pressures of time mean that small groups and the whole class will sometimes need to carry out activities related to secretarial and presentational issues that have arisen in the course of writing workshop.

- Children who are struggling must be identified early and given more support.

This is often signalled by a reluctance to put words on paper and is regularly accompanied by an insistence that words must always be spelled 'correctly'. The child needs to be taught the spellings of a core of commonly used words. This may be supported by phonetic strategies and visual strategies; however, the teacher still needs to encourage the child to invent other spellings. The consequences for the child of not being prepared to invent spellings are restricted written vocabulary, and difficulties for the teacher in attempting to interact positively in the context of the child's written work.

- Teachers' strategies when hearing children read should be part of a continuum between an emphasis on learning to read, and critical discussions on reading and texts. They are dependent on the individual child and the context.

During writing conference the teacher must prioritize the features of the writing that the child must attend to. In order to do this, the teacher needs a clear understanding of the distinction between composition and transcription. The teacher's interaction will be directly influenced by their knowledge of the child, previous support offered, the nature of the piece of writing, the stage in the year etc.

- Higher order reading is actively developed, particularly through the teacher's expert choice of texts and their knowledge of the issues such texts generate.

More experienced writers are encouraged to attempt more and more demanding tasks that extend their thinking skills. These are some suggestions for such tasks that teachers have tried: those children who develop significant expertise in story writing are encouraged to develop expertise in non-fiction forms; those children who produce a wide range of forms at a high level might be offered additional special projects such as the editorship of a school magazine or a link with another school, where the interests of the reader must be surveyed and reflected in the writing of a book; the suggestion to research a topic of interest may include subject areas outside the child's normal experience, such as the mystery surrounding John F. Kennedy; a survey of children's preferences for mathematics activities could be investigated, collated, written up and presented during sharing time. Teachers can also create such tasks by translating their professional reading into classroom activities. For example, the continuing interest in the writing of argument could usefully be explored.

By looking at the links between the real book approach and the process approach, it has been possible to identify some directions for future practice. Reading still seems to attract a greater amount of interest in terms of research, publication and media attention. This seems to neglect the importance of primary writing. Perhaps if more attention was paid to writing there would be positive benefits for the teaching and learning of reading in addition to the benefits for writing.

EIGHT

Developing the process approach throughout the school

In order for the process approach to have the maximum benefit for the children in the school it needs to be adopted as an aspect of whole school policy; this means a commitment by all educators in the school. The achievement of this aim is not an easy task, and the responsibility falls to a large extent on the language coordinator.

The importance of a motivated, informed, energetic and effective language coordinator cannot be emphasized enough. The language and English curriculum has always been complex and controversial, and will continue to be so. It is also a curriculum area that impinges on many others, directly and indirectly. It is for these reasons that the role of the language coordinator is such a demanding one. The poor level of funding that primary schools receive often results in the language coordinator having to do their job with very little non-contact time. In the light of recent intense criticism of primary education in some quarters, it seems unjust that primary schools continue to experience such funding problems in comparison to other educational institutions. How are coordinators supposed to monitor the language curriculum and support colleagues' professional development without the time to work with them in the classroom?

If it is accepted that whole school agreement is important, the language coordinator, in collaboration with colleagues, needs to evaluate the current position of the school in terms of language development. Following this review, plans need to be made to extend or develop 'living' language policies. If the school is committed to encouraging more use of the process approach, I believe that the process of school development and policy making itself should mirror the philosophies behind the process approach. The implication is that policy development should be school centred, offering teachers some control over the issues that are covered both during the INSET programme and in the policy itself.

This chapter draws on my own experience as a language coordinator, developing, implementing, and monitoring language policies in two contrasting schools. During this work the process approach was both a subject for discussion and an influence on the structure of the policy development. The chapter begins with descriptions of four INSET meetings that were held, two in Catton First School and two in Gallack Primary School. The examples illustrate how language coordinators can begin the process of discussion and start to develop the process approach throughout the school. The examples also show how two different school staffs responded. I compare similar INSET meetings in order to illustrate the different responses from the two staffs. The first comparison involves a meeting to set the agendas for policy development of the writing curriculum. The second comparison illustrates meetings that looked at an aspect of the development of reading. An additional outcome of adopting a process-based framework for the policy development was the emergence of a planning framework for INSET programmes. The chapter concludes with an analysis of three language policy documents.

Comparison one – agenda setting

The first INSET meeting in both schools was an agenda setting one. This was a brainstorm where staff identified issues that they felt needed addressing during the process of INSET and policy development. At this stage all contributions were recorded on flipcharts. It was not intended to prioritize at the beginning of the meeting. As the meeting progressed, priorities were agreed and these priorities reflected the themes of future INSET and the structure of the policy document.

The staff at Catton First School prioritized the following issues for the writing curriculum: 'philosophy of language teaching; what is writing?; when does writing begin?; physical organization of the classroom; activities; strategies; child choice; composition; spelling – strategies and issues'. One of the interesting aspects of the priorities was the importance that the teachers attached to a shared philosophy of the teaching of language. The teachers thought that these underlying philosophies were important if a shared approach was to be achieved in practice.

In a subsequent meeting the staff discussed philosophies and arrived at a list that they felt summed up the most important features of the teaching and learning of language at the school. The list was included in the language policy file, and had implications beyond the language curriculum.

Teaching centred around children's needs
Looking for the positive
Belief in children's desire to make sense of the world
The importance of talk
High expectations for success
Children learn by doing
The curriculum must be informed by issues of justice and equality
Children learn by 'the company they keep'
Education involves communities not just schools
The most effective learning is that controlled by the child

Children cannot learn unless they are self confident
We want children working for their own satisfaction not for crude rewards

The staff of Gallack Primary School also identified a range of issues that were to be used as the themes for INSET meetings. The process of prioritization resulted in the framework shown in Table 8.1.

As language coordinator I grouped the issues that the staff identified under broad headings or themes that were to be the basis of the INSET programme. The range of issues that was identified under each theme reflected the staff's opinion of what needed to be covered during the policy work. Within each theme certain issues were further prioritized to ensure that the programme of development covered areas that were of most importance.

As can be seen from the section on composition, the process approach was to be explicitly covered during the policy work. In this particular case, writing workshop attracted much interest. Some of the teachers who had reservations about some of the proposed changes to the language curriculum were enthused by the possibilities for writing workshop. In addition to this explicit coverage, the collaborative agenda setting for the teachers mirrored the

Table 8.1   Brainstorm of agendas for INSET meetings

The beginnings of writing
Emergent literacy; letter name v letter sound; invented spelling; scribble v mark making; case studies of individual children; the philosophy of;

Form
The range of forms; expressive, transactional and poetic modes; teaching poetry; how story develops through the primary school;

Composition
What is a writing workshop?; bookmaking/publishing in the classroom; extending writing; brainstorming; drafting; when is copy-writing appropriate?; audience; balance in teacher interaction;

Transcription
Presentation; handwriting scheme; when to join up; development of spelling; punctuation; use of pens/pencils etc.; using the computer;

Equal opportunities
Multilingualism; gender and use of the computer; dominance of teacher time; literacy recovery programmes; how do we know when an approach is not working?; differentiation;

Classroom organization
Teaching strategies; responding to children's writing; resources;

Knowledge about language
Languages children speak in the school; what do we mean by grammar?; dialect and accent; use of language in different contexts; standard English; sentence construction;

Recording achievements
The Primary Language Record; shared understandings

---

brainstorming that one might have with children during a mini-lesson at the start of a writing workshop session.

A similar approach was taken with the teaching of reading, where lists of priorities were agreed. In the following section I take the curriculum development process a little further and describe two of the meetings that resulted from the prioritization, and the different staffs' responses.

Comparison two – looking at reading

Both schools had a meeting to review the reading resources that were available in the school. During the meeting, reading scheme books were compared with other books, and both sets were examined for their continuing relevance for the children. I wrote short reviews that were clipped inside the real books in order to raise important issues such as higher order thinking skills, detecting stereotype and bias, influences etc. The following example was clipped inside *Where The Wild Things Are* by Maurice Sendak.

Where The Wild Things Are – Maurice Sendak

A classic literary picture book. Deals with a subject close to any child's heart – naughtiness. Although the child gets the punishment he deserves, Mum still loves him. (There was an attempt to rewrite the Beatrix Potter stories in a new modern format. The publishers tried to replace natural consequences of misbehaviour with strongly moralistic endings. They weren't very popular.) Notice how the first sentence spans three pages and has a complex clause structure which many children eagerly respond to. This perhaps calls into question attempts to artificially simplify sentence structure and vocabulary in the mistaken belief that all children need this. The pictures grow progressively bigger, emphasizing the structure, until the main event of the story is represented by six pages of pictures without text. The story also has a cyclic structure common to many art forms. The end is minimalist, just five words and no picture.

The two schools responded in quite different ways to this activity. Catton School already had a commitment to the use of a range of high quality fiction, although the *Story Chest* reading scheme was available. In addition there were examples of several other schemes. The feelings expressed at this meeting resulted in this school adopting 'real' books as their main resource for the teaching of reading. The majority of teachers in the school were happy to adopt this policy decision, partly because they felt a sense of ownership, and because of their philosophical commitment to progressive practice. Here is a selection of their reactions to the books.

Reading scheme books
- A high proportion of middle class environments depicted and the absence of British-Asian or British-AfroCaribbean faces.
- The content of the texts seemed to have little relevance to the children at the school.

- The language used in the texts was unnatural.
- It made no difference if some of the books were read backwards.

Other books
- The language in the real books was relevant to the children.
- The illustrations were often outstanding examples of accurate and creative visual art.
- The books would motivate children.

When a similar meeting was held in the second school it was agreed that a minority of children might not need the structure of the reading scheme and that some could miss out various sections. The school had used a selection of reading schemes in a more structured way for many years. The first consequence of the school's approach was the lack of opportunity the teachers had to evaluate books other than reading scheme books. Their professional expertise was restricted by the previous policy. Like the children, they had only had limited opportunity to debate the literary consequences and issues raised by high quality fiction. It was recognized that teachers needed to interact using the 'real' books as well as the scheme books if the children were to get the most positive learning experiences.

Partly to challenge the essence of this activity, and what the staff reasonably perceived to be an underlying agenda, the teachers made the point that perhaps it was not a fair comparison because the most recent schemes were not available to compare. One teacher commented on the kinds of issue raised in the reviews by questioning the merits of encouraging higher order thinking skills at the expense of reading for pleasure. In answer to this it was suggested that the two concepts were not necessarily mutually exclusive. One of the surprising findings to emerge from this meeting was that despite limited selections of high quality children's literature available in classroom reading areas, the teachers reserved their interaction for the reading scheme books only. One of the underlying issues for the meetings on reading was related to decisions on the use of the process approach. The feeling that the school needed to move towards some of the philosophies associated with real books was mirrored by discussions about the adoption of the process approach to writing.

The four meetings that I have described tackled aspects of language policy development by taking a school centred approach. The process approach was both an issue of content during the meetings and also a theoretical foundation that influenced the process of policy development itself. Adoption of the process approach has benefits not only for children but also for teacher professional development. In the following section I give an example of such development. The framework I present emerged as both a tool for language coordinators and a means to reflect further on policy development that focuses on the process approach.

The INSET meeting framework

The work in the schools represented extended periods of language policy development over a number of years. An important part of this development was the programme of INSET meetings where important issues were debated and consensus reached. Some time after the work in the two schools I read through the notes I had kept and reflected upon the format of the meetings that I had organized. Although the school centred approach to policy development produced different priorities and hence different meetings, there were distinct similarities. Rather than look in depth at the content of the meetings, I speculated that the formats of the meetings might offer a pattern or framework that would support any future planning. I felt that if I could identify a framework, this might be useful for other coordinators who were thinking about the format of INSET meetings when developing the school's approach to writing and language.

Each section of the diagram is a key word for an INSET meeting format. Classroom practice is central to the diagram, but underlying educational philosophies in the outer circle represent the way that all other aspects are affected by teachers' beliefs and philosophies. The inner circle demonstrates the importance of staff ownership of meeting agendas if 'living' policies are to be achieved. The line and arrow through the middle of the diagram

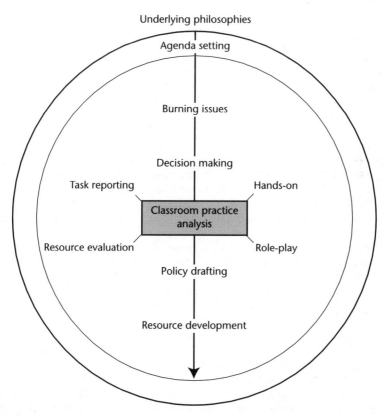

Figure 8.1 Formats for curriculum development meetings

represent the process of development from discussion of important issues through to the written draft of the policy. The descriptions of the keywords that follow draw on my experience of delivering such meetings.

Underlying philosophies

Ideally at least one meeting needs to tackle the curriculum and pedagogy at this level, for example, looking at the importance placed on research and professional reading in the school, or 'why is teamwork and shared practice desirable?' The number of meetings needed for this topic will vary according to how far the school already has agreement on philosophies. A series of statements based on staff attitudes to education were used where staff had to indicate degrees of agreement or disagreement. Staff worked first in pairs, then fours, and finally as the full staff group. At each stage the group had to reach consensus.

Agenda setting

Here the coordinator encourages staff to make decisions on the issues to be addressed through the INSET programme. To help colleagues to set the agenda, I offered open brainstorming sessions and/or semi-structured plans which gave some ideas but encouraged staff to add their own. The coordinator may need to add to staff suggestions to ensure breadth. For example, if 'phonics' is requested as an issue for discussion, the coordinator might want to include reference to syntactics and semantics in the meeting.

Burning issues

These are contentious issues which can serve to ignite the process of discussion and reflection. They are often topics which come up in informal discussions, such as the place of reading schemes, spelling tests, decontextualized testing, grammar etc. They can serve to encourage people to state their honest views on a particular subject. If used too often, this category can lead to time-wasting over issues where fundamental disagreement lies and where agreement to differ is more constructive. The use of spelling tests is an example where discussion about their use can detract from more constructive debate which might brainstorm the multitude of other strategies that are possible to support the development of spelling.

Classroom practice analysis

This is arguably the most important aspect of staff development. Teachers reflect on their own practice in a variety of contexts. The ideal medium here is audiovisual presentation of practice taking place in the school, which teachers can then discuss. Some colleagues, however, find the use of their own work an uncomfortable experience, so professionally produced materials can be used instead. The coordinator's work could also be videoed for discussion. Shared discussion in pairs or small groups rather than with the complete staff group can also help to produce discussion in a less daunting atmosphere. I used a video produced by the LINC project which showed a primary teacher reading with a child in her class. This enabled the staff to highlight aspects of interaction which we felt were important.

Task reporting

Teachers offer information on new approaches that they have tried in the classroom. This is a useful way to encourage constructive feedback based on a fair evaluation. This format can avoid the problems with 'lip-service', where teachers sometimes voice enthusiasm over a new initiative but are reluctant to evaluate it in their classroom – for example the comparison of pieces of writing which show how invented spelling is progressing in the classroom.

Resource evaluation

Useful group debate can be stimulated by staff evaluation of alternative teaching materials. I encouraged staff to write comments about a range of new reading schemes on a pro-forma also designed to further extend thinking. These comments provided further evidence of the issues that teachers felt were important. Resources are often an important indicator of school philosophies and approach.

Hands-on

Various practical activities can be experienced by teachers with a view to reflecting on their classroom practice and the likely benefits for children. Teachers experiencing 'writing workshop' approaches where everyone has the opportunity to write freely and share with colleagues afterwards, can be a powerful experience.

Role-play

This can be an opportunity for teachers to confront some of their inhibitions and, in so doing, reflect deeper on their practice and the practice of others. One of the scenarios included enacting the role of an irate parent who was suggesting that teachers never 'corrected' her child's work. Trio exercises were also used, where teachers worked in threes and played the roles of speaker, listener and observer where they talked about 'views on the teaching of literacy'. This obliged them to articulate their beliefs and identify philosophical frameworks.

Decision making

There comes a point when exploratory discussions must turn to decisions on policy. It is necessary to set a time limit for these and produce extracts of the policy for staff to amend. Later in the chapter I look at some examples of school policies.

It can be seen from my description of the key words from the diagram that each key word can suggest a number of meetings. As with any classification, the categories are not always unique to one format. Often, meetings would draw on several of the key words. The key words 'decision-making' perhaps represent one of the most challenging stages of policy development. In an ideal situation each meeting should produce a number of policy decisions; in practice this is not always the case. The coordinator is always trying to ensure that discussion is productive and leads towards definite decisions on school practice.

Policy documents

The drafting of the policy document is an important process in itself. At this stage colleagues are encouraged to add, or suggest changes, to the policy document. The aim is to establish agreement on the approach to language and literacy development throughout the school. The policy document must describe classroom practice and illustrate achievable targets so that teachers and others can check that the policy is being adopted. If this is the case, a policy of general statements that fits onto one side of A4 is not going to be acceptable. If the policy is to be a 'living' document it should also reflect the issues that were covered during INSET. It acts as a record of the process as well as a statement of current practice.

Hann (1996: 6) takes a different view of policy documents. He claims that in the past, 'language policies were often lengthy documents, with recommended practical approaches submerged in detailed discussion of quotations from various educationists of influence'. Hann suggests that a better approach is to adopt the ideas of Caldwell and Spinks (1988). They suggest that the policy document should comprise a number of sections suitable for the different audiences. (It is interesting to note that the children themselves are rarely included as members of such audiences.) Caldwell and Spinks suggest that governors will require a straightforward outline. This should be one sheet of A4 for writing, one for reading, and one for talking. They advise that teachers will require more detailed guidance, and that this may be represented in the form of bullet points. Having separate sections for the different readers seems to be a useful idea; however, I do not think that all the language and literacy issues that schools reach agreement on can be covered by bullet points alone.

Although Hann is critical of past policy documents that were insufficiently practical, I feel that it is important that research and theory underpin the practical decisions that are taken during the period of policy development. Too many primary teachers regard their own personal experience as the only justification for pedagogical decisions. All teachers and schools' should be encouraged to look for a view outside the classroom in order to justify and challenge their own practice. It follows that these outside views should be part of the policy document. Hann paradoxically points out that 'Subscribing to journals such as *Language Matters* is not a luxury in a period when resources may be limited: they are important sources of information for coordinators in advising about current issues and on further resource acquisition.'

Dougill (1993) takes an alternative view to Hann. He suggests that the language policy might be contained in a ring binder to facilitate any changes in the school's thinking or approach. (One aspect of policy development that is sometimes neglected is the need to set a date for review of the policy, in order to evaluate and reflect on the things that are progressing well and those that need to be changed.) Dougill offers a wider range of areas that might be addressed by the language policy.

- A statement of principles of procedure . . . This would identify the style of learning the school wishes to underpin its language development work.
- Suggestions of successful learning/teaching strategies and how they were set up.
- Examples of children's work and teacher-produced booklets, worksheets and so on.
- How to plan for progression and continuity.
- The evaluation of the policy in practice.
- The criteria used for the selection of resources.
- The concepts, skills and attitudes which are to be developed.
- How children's progress is to be monitored and assessed.
- Key learning experiences planned for pupils.
- Lists of resources and addresses and so on.
- Important articles from journals or extracts from books.
- Policy statements on issues like:
  - the library
  - multi-cultural education
  - what children should know about language
  - drama
  - media education
  - etc.

(Dougill 1993: 101)

Within this range I do think that elements of classroom practice need to be clearly defined so that teachers, coordinators and headteachers can monitor curriculum practice effectively.

Policy extracts

School 1

The final part of this chapter gives extracts from the writing policies of three schools and illustrates the implications of some of their decisions. (Appendix 2 gives full lists of contents for these policies.) One school felt that the physical organization of the classroom was a particularly important aspect of their practice. Following a staff meeting to discuss some of the implications for the classroom, a number of decisions were taken that were included in the policy document:

Practicalities

Physical organization of the classroom

We support the use of a clearly defined 'writing area' within all class-rooms, in addition to other areas of the classroom children may choose or be encouraged to write in. The resources for the area should include a variety of writing implements, ideally present continually, but over a period of time would still be valuable. Similarly a range of different sizes, colours and types of paper including made-up booklets and more sophisti-cated book making equipment. Vertical displays in the area need to have a variety of written examples including children's work, different scripts, environmental print, alphabets, etc. If the area is to be successful teachers need to consider how often they go there, the nature of their interaction and how children are using the area.

Role-play areas in classrooms are also an important way of encourag-ing children to write. An office is an obvious example where typewriters, phones and memo pads, notebooks, stamps, forms, etc. are all useful. A travel agency with brochures, tickets, passports, hotel guides, phrase-books and so on. A hospital; market stalls . . .

Each child can have a writing folder. It gives children a reminder of their history as a writer and is also a sensible way for children to control the various bits of writing they start and finish at different times from each other. It is a good basis for negotiating work to be part of the child's portfolio which goes forward to other teachers. It can also have labels stuck on as an aid to contributing to the process of recording the child's achievements as a writer. E.g. Writing I have finished; books I have pub-lished; composition/transcription concepts I have learned.

Classroom publishing is a vital part of any language learning situation. Books are a large part of this. If publication is a regular and natural exten-sion of a child's written ideas many things can be learned by going through the process. Simple booklets and the materials for making them should be available all the time in the writing area. More elaborate books from groups and/or individuals can be written whenever possible and again, if practical, the materials should be available all the time. Some books should become part of the class reading area. One individual pub-lished book for each child per year is a realistic minimum target.

One of the important parts of learning the transcription (secretary) side of writing concerns motor control and holding the pencil. It is easy to forget that a significant proportion of children are left handed. Ultimately, how children sit, the position of their paper and how they hold the pencil are important issues when you consider the immense physical effort involved in writing. The contribution of play experience is vital. Fine and gross motor skills will be developed through a range of play experiences in the early years.

As a constant reminder and reference point for primary children *all* classrooms should have a clearly visible alphabet frieze in English and other languages.

Writing workshops are a very good way to focus on the process of writing. Donald Graves popularized this way of working and his book *Writing: children and teachers at work* is a fine introduction. Basically his ideas start from a whole class writing together (including the teacher). Everybody decides what they write and how they write it. The writing folder facilitates this over time as it is an on-going process. Writers have discussions ('conferences') with the teacher and other children about their writing in the middle of a number of drafts. Sharing writing is very important to this way of working and classroom publishing facilitates this.

This example of a policy document written in 1991 raises a number of issues. The policy was put together in a ringbound folder with colour coding for the different sections. Policy statements such as the one above were copied on one colour; practically orientated support materials were another colour, and theoretical material was another colour. Once the policy had been established the teachers found that the amount of time they spent in the writing area and the quality of their interaction seemed to influence the quality of the writing and the children's motivation to use the writing area. The teachers also started to monitor how often children chose to use the area. This helped them to balance teacher direction with child choice.

The extract does identify clear targets for practice. For example: 'One individual published book for each child per year is a realistic minimum target' or 'As a constant reminder and reference point for primary children *all* class-rooms should have a clearly visible alphabet frieze in English and other languages.' However, because the policy is not just a series of bullet points it is able to touch on some of the complexities of language and literacy. The teaching and learning of language is not always clear cut; there are areas where the identification of simple targets may not reflect the genuine complexities that exist. The style of the policy also allowed for more tentative statements, based on a recognition that all schools are continually developing and that research knowledge about language and literacy is also continually developing.

In the extract, only Donald Graves is referred to as a possible source of further reading. I believe that policies should contain references to research that supports the school's position where possible. Clearly this is difficult for coordinators if they do not have easy access to such resources. However, the advisory services and local universities should be able to support the coordinator in this respect. For example, the policy states, 'The contribution of play experience is vital.' This kind of statement could have referred to research that supported it.

School 2

The second school had a well established procedure for supporting writing in the early years. However, the headteacher felt that aspects of this practice needed to change. One of the first difficulties the language coordinator experienced was finding out how the current approach worked. The philosophies and much of the practice seemed to have emerged over a number of years and had not been made explicit. In addition there was some resistance to the process of change. Some teachers saw the policy development process merely as a way of describing current practice and writing it down, rather than as a process of evaluation and development. Because of this debate the language coordinator felt it necessary to use the policy document partly as a statement of current practice but also as a means of pushing forward the process of change.

The beginnings of writing

At Key Stage 1 a balance is achieved between clearly structured tasks and approaches which develop certain essential skills, and approaches which foster 'emergent literacy'. Children are taught the important sounds associated with letters, and the names of the letters right from the start of school. The phonic links are developed a little and often, sometimes using a flipchart with the whole class, often on a one to one basis while discussing a piece of the child's writing, and by regularly reading aloud and discussing poems, songs and rhymes which rely on phonic patterns for their rhymes. The important thing is that children learn that there is a general link between sound and symbol which they can go on to learn for themselves. It is not possible or desirable to try and teach all the sound symbol relationships. For example the 'e' in 'remember' has three different sounds. This could be confusing to the child who has been taught that 'e' sounds like the 'e' in 'get'.

Our 'emergent literacy' approaches involve expecting children to write, 'scribble' or generally make their own marks as soon as they enter school. The teacher then encourages the child to read what they have written and interacts with the child, often rewriting what the child has written in standard English. Our approach also involves helping children to write their own books independently. Sometimes they may work with another child, or the teacher might act as scribe for their story, or they might be encouraged to record onto tape which can then be transcribed.

There is a large amount of research which shows that when all children first enter nursery or reception they bring with them a wide range of literacy and language skills/knowledge. With some children it can take great skill on the teacher's part to recognize the children's positive pre-school achievements. To give children the opportunity to show this we regularly offer them the opportunity to 'mark-make' and write freely, either in the writing corner/area or in role play areas specially designed to encourage literacy, e.g. travel agent, doctor's surgery, office, home corner, etc. Teachers interact with children during these activities.

To develop the concept of words and spaces, regularly used words are displayed on the classroom walls. These will be written on a variety of pictures to encourage the children to recognize the difference between them and to help the teacher point them out to the child. Environmental print will be used wherever possible by referring to food packaging, clothing labels, text on children's toys, etc. Local visits give an opportunity to photograph print on advertisements, road signs, shops, etc. and to plan activities in the classroom using this knowledge.

Often the early years teacher will act as 'scribe'. This may be a shared writing session where a group of children all contribute to a story and the teacher writes it on a flipchart or easel. Often the teacher will be responding to independent writing the child has done and she/he will want to model the standard form of writing. Sometimes the children will be paired up so they can work on one text between them. At other times the computer is a useful tool for encouraging writing and redrafting.

This policy document was written during the school year 1993/94. The first difference to note is the identification of key stages. The first school policy seemed to describe the development of language as something that was more developmental than age related. The National Curriculum clearly influenced the second school, but I think that a difference in philosophy is also evident.

The voice of the coordinator and/or possibly the headteacher seems to be evident in the document in a way that encourages the process of change. Stylistically this sometimes sits a little uncomfortably. The policy document is not a simple statement of the practice that should be evident in the school, but it is also attempting to improve practice. An example of this stylistic variation comes in the following lines:

> The important thing is that children learn that there is a general link between sound and symbol which they can go on to learn for themselves. It is not possible or desirable to try and teach all the sound symbol relationships. For example the 'e' in 'remember' has three different sounds. This could be confusing to the child who has been taught that 'e' sounds like the 'e' in 'get'.

There is a shift from the language of policy statement to the language associated with changing classroom practice.

The notion that the individual child's generalizations are important is similar to Mudd's (1994) views on spelling outlined in Chapter 4. The practice of linking pictures with words other than nouns is also interesting. One of the problems with teaching these words in the early years is that they do not have a picture that can be simply linked with them. The teachers decided to link these common words with pictures and stick them on the wall simply as a visual reference point. Some teachers might argue that the use of pictures is perhaps unnecessary, and that the children should learn to see the word itself as a visual shape rather than have to link it with a picture.

School 3

The final example of a school policy was written in 1996; it forms part of the language policy for an infant school. The school had used the process approach for a number of years, but it was felt that the policy documentation should be reviewed. The section of the policy devoted to writing was divided into three parts: writing, spelling and handwriting. This reflected the divisions of the National Curriculum. The example below is from the section titled 'writing'.

Aims

We intend to foster self expression, to enable the child to communicate effectively in a variety of different written styles.

Objectives

Self expression. The child is able to communicate in writing.
The child is able to record and share information with others.
The child is able to write in various modes and select the most suitable for the task.
The child has a sense of authorship by being able to 'publish' pieces of written work.
The child has a purpose for writing.

The role of the teacher

Children develop a sense of the variety of written language if writing is a purposeful activity (e.g. when the role-play area is used as a travel agency or post office). They can also see how writing should be tackled by watching adults writing, by having help from adults as scribes, and writing alongside them, and by being given choices of subject matter, writing materials, conditions and time.

The conventions of letter formation, spelling and punctuation all need to be taught. They should be introduced to help the expression of meaning. Effective teaching of writing depends upon the ability of the teacher to identify when the child needs support and advice in order to make further progress.

We have identified a number of different stages the children might reach in the emergent writing continuum. Not all children will progress neatly from one stage to the next, and sometimes a plateau is reached. The continuum is to act as a reference point for the teacher when looking at the written work of the children. A copy of this is included in the guidelines.

Initial efforts – marks on a page – will be followed by writing which is characterized by invented spelling, letter formation and partial understanding of many of the conventions of English. We start from where the children are at, believing they are writers and move on from there.

It is important to introduce drafting and collaboration to encourage planning and critical reading.

The teacher needs to be a praiser of achievement and effort, a standard setter and an editorial consultant for the children.

The computer can be used in the writing process. Children should be encouraged to write directly onto the computer using programs such as 'Pendown' and 'Phases'. 'Desktop Stories' has a library of pictures that the children can call on to write about and then produce their own text, thereby creating a book.

Children should be encouraged to see writing as something that has to be worked on in order to produce a final draft. They need to be given the time and the space to work on ideas. There are a number of little books ready for the children to present their finished work in, and these are then displayed in the library areas and borrowed by other children.

One of the interesting aspects of the extract is the way the child is at the centre of the description of practice. The other policy examples tended to focus on the work of teachers. In the last extract, examples of this child-centred approach to policy writing include: 'Children develop a sense . . .'; 'identify when the child needs support . . .'; 'not all children will progress neatly . . .'. The constant reference to the needs of the children in the school is a refreshing emphasis to be expressed in a language policy.

The role of the teacher is summed up by the following phrase: 'The teacher needs to be a praiser of achievement and effort, a standard setter and an editorial consultant for the children.' This seems to identify some of the most important aspects of the teacher's role. The importance of a specific positive outlook on all aspects of children's learning is clearly signalled. This comes alongside the recognition that achievement will vary from child to child and will be based on effort. The words 'editorial consultant' suggest the kind of relationship that is so important during writing workshop, where there is a two-way process of teaching and learning taking place.

The reference to use of word processing software is significant. The software is not seen as a means of practising skills and drills, but as a tool that supports the process of writing. The publication cycle is clearly a part of the children's experiences; 'Desktop Stories' has a library of pictures that the children can call on to write about and then produce their own text, thereby creating a book.

It has been seen from the examples of policy documents from three schools that the process approach formed part of classroom and school practice. Teachers need to be given encouragement to evaluate the use of the approach in the classroom so that they are in a better position to understand its use. Policy work should enable teachers to have this experience and should include the process approach as part of policy documentation.

This chapter has placed the process approach in the wider context of policy development. This is important because any approach to language and literacy should not be seen as an isolated example of classroom practice. If children are not to be confused, and if continuity and progression is an issue for schools, teachers must share many aspects of their practice. This should not preclude individual teachers developing particular enthusiasms and expertise, but it should mean that children receive a core approach that is linked by sound theories.

NINE

The process approach and the National Curriculum

The roots of the process approach come from two primary sources: the practice of teachers that caused them to reflect on traditional teaching and learning techniques; and at the same time, researchers such as Donald Graves, who attempted to look at the work of teachers and children and suggest directions for future practice. Both these roots were sustained by the motivation of the teachers and researchers concerned. This motivation came partly from the knowledge that they had the power to change the curriculum and pedagogy in line with their view of the needs of the children they worked with.

In the UK the development of a National Curriculum has had a profound effect on the time that teachers have to evaluate teaching methods. The authoritarian approach to curriculum reform has resulted in reduced motivation and energy to try different approaches. Prior to 1988 there was no National Curriculum, although the idea had been raised a number of times, and most memorably by James Callaghan in his Ruskin College speech at Oxford. Without a National Curriculum, teachers and schools made their own decisions concerning curriculum and pedagogy, supported by local education authorities and professional bodies. The positive side of this was the freedom and scope that teachers had to investigate the curriculum and methods of teaching, and to evaluate their potential. The negative side was that there was a danger that continuity, progression and equal access to the curriculum could have been endangered because of the lack of a national structure.

The fact that this chapter exists at all is a recognition that the National Curriculum places a burden of responsibility on all teachers. However, it is important to retain a sense of perspective; it is important to evaluate the National Curriculum just as rigorously as we would evaluate any other statement of policy and/or practice. If teachers and schools know their pupils' learning needs best, it follows that sometimes national documentation may not represent accurately what is the most appropriate curriculum content or the best ways of helping children to learn. If this is the case, teachers need to use the National Curriculum as a tool which can be used to justify aspects of effective practice and theory. The National Curriculum should not be viewed uncriti-cally just because the law instructs that it must be followed. This is important as a general philosophy, but especially in the light of the review of the National Curriculum that is due in the year 2000.

In the spirit of the last statement, I offer a personal view of the most recent version of the English section of the National Curriculum. Following the Kingman and Cox reports, the original English document was generally regarded as a useful outline of much good practice that was already evident in many schools. However, since then the work of Sir Ron Dearing has resulted in a shorter version. The first part of this chapter is a critique of the current National Curriculum English document. The final part of the chapter analy-ses this documentation to illustrate how the use of the process approach is related to the National Curriculum English requirements.

The National Curriculum – a personal critique

When analysing the National Curriculum it is important to keep in mind the history of its development, as this offers a sense of perspective. In 1987 Kenneth Baker published the 'consultation' papers for the original National Curriculum; however, he chose not to publish the responses. In spite of the timing of the consultation – during the summer holidays – 20,000 responses were received. Julian Haviland (1988) collected some of these responses in his book *Take Care, Mr Baker!* and he highlights the response given by 'The Cam-paign for the Advancement of State Education' which he says was represen-tative.

> None of the documents makes any mention of the effects the proposed changes will have on present pupils of our schools, their teachers or on the role and responsibilities of headteachers. None draws on either experi-ence or research to inform the ideas contained in them. There is a funda-mental inconsistency in the proposals which is so blatant that we must look to the political philosophy which has generated them to find an explanation.
>
> (Haviland 1988: 5)

National documentation offers a dilemma for teachers and coordinators. Nationally prescribed curricula may offer uniformity, but this can result in cur-riculum debate which teachers find rather dull. I believe that curriculum reform works best when coordinators link good practice, research, staff views and their own professional interests in order to motivate colleagues, resulting in initiatives which really do affect children's learning.

Good practice in the conception and delivery of INSET would suggest that shared agenda setting, where staff offer important areas for professional development, is vital to retain staff motivation and produce language policies which are living documents used by all colleagues. Underpinning this approach to school development is the implication that teachers will nomi-nate issues which directly affect them; unfortunately these issues do not necessarily accord with national frameworks for the curriculum. The repeated inadequacy of national consultation has resulted in rejection by teachers, most memorably in primary teachers' rejection of the original flawed testing and assessment model.

Overall the division of the document into three sections, Range, Key Skills, and Standard English and Language Study, seems more straightforward than the previous forms. One of my main criticisms of previous documentation has been the constantly changing layouts not only between orders but between different subjects as well. The notion of level descriptors also seems a reasonable one; however, the descriptions are not firmly rooted in teacher observation of children's language behaviour. Because of this there are difficulties in interpretation. Having said that, I would not want to see a return to the original teacher moderation process, which attempted unsuccessfully to moderate complex aspects of child development.

As far as the detailed requirements are concerned, the issue for teachers and coordinators is, do they support good practice and can they be used to strengthen the process of curriculum reform? It is good to see that speaking and listening still has an equal place in the language/English curriculum; however, the programme of study is rather vague compared with those for reading and writing. I think the place of oracy in the curriculum still needs better understanding, as clearly it is delivered quite differently from reading and writing. From my own classroom experience I believe that some of the important aspects of oracy include the grouping of children, awareness of gender, lateral thinking and problem solving, raising awareness of bilingualism, collaborative skills, language acquisition, links with parents and the community etc. These kinds of specific reference are absent.

Looking at reading, one can see the possible influence of the theories of 'real book' approaches. At KS1 there are requirements to teach pupils: to become 'enthusiastic, responsive and knowledgeable' readers; that illustrations are 'visually stimulating', 'use of language that benefits from being read aloud and reread'; and at KS2 that they read for their 'own interest and pleasure'. Many of these principles were also enshrined in the early English documentation, and publishers have found that reading schemes which have inappropriately controlled vocabularies, uninteresting texts, stereotypic illustrations etc. perhaps do not fulfil the letter of the law; hence the rush of publishers to offer new improved reading schemes. Having inspected several of them I was struck by the greater range of texts they now offer and how some of the publicity material contains language that would not be out of place in texts on learning to read with real books. The challenge for some coordinators will be to come to terms with the change in philosophy implied by the National Curriculum, as research on the subject seems to suggest that a minimum of 95 per cent of schools use formal reading schemes (Gray 1983; Rice 1987; Cato *et al.* 1992).

In spite of the enhanced priority given to phonics in the document, the other cueing strategies are recognized. Marie Clay's focus on semantic, syntactic and graphophonic cueing strategies, and Kenneth Goodman's work on miscue analysis, is now well known. However, for some reason the document refers to semantic cueing as 'contextual' clues. This seems misleading; as all four cueing systems rely on the reading context, 'semantic' would have been a better term. At Key Stage 2 it is good to see references to the study of media and drama; yet in spite of HMI concerns about the teaching of higher order thinking skills at Key Stage 2, the key skills and range of this area are rather unspecific. References to reading reviews, reading between the lines, critical responses, awareness of sexism and racism in texts etc. would have provided more concrete guidance.

Writing

The importance of emergent literacy approaches and writing workshop are supported by the statement that 'pupils should be taught to write independently on subjects that are of interest to them' and 'pupils' early experiments and independent attempts at communicating in writing, using letters and known words, should be encouraged'. However, the early emphasis on 'using letters and known words' could marginalize the importance of the mark making and letter strings stages that early writers usually pass through. Regrettably, the importance of pupils writing about things that interest them seems to disappear at Key Stage 2. It seems to me that the importance of writing workshop and classroom publishing approaches become even greater at Key Stage 2, as pupils can make informed choices in terms of written form and style.

As in earlier documentation, the distinction between key skills in composition as opposed to transcription is not made clearly enough. Frank Smith (1982) provides a powerful argument for the clear separation of the two concepts at different stages of the writing process (see Chapter 3). The constituent parts of written compositional development still seem to be a difficult area for primary teachers to conceptualize, and they receive little clarity from the document.

The important link between standard spelling and semantics is made clear, and this is useful, as HMI have pointed out that older pupils make many spelling errors by selecting the wrong word meaning. However, the way that good spellers learn to understand the limitations of phonetic spelling strategies is not referred to. There seems to be a lack of clarity with regard to the appropriate development of phonetic understanding, and the specific differences in skills and concepts that exist when encoding a piece of writing as opposed to decoding a text.

Overall the document may have given teachers a small sense of satisfaction to see that – following the draft proposals – their recommendations for change seemed to have been taken on board. References to media work, the balance of reading strategies, less aggressive language on standard English etc. were all modified thanks to responses from many people in education. However, there are still omissions, such as the lack of reference to the specific needs of bilingual children. These needs are such important issues for so many teachers that I find it remarkable that the document makes precious little reference to the specific key skills and range that might benefit these pupils.

It can be seen from my critique that there are a number of areas that are still unsatisfactory. Part of the problem lies in the attempt to reduce the complexity of language and literacy development to such a short document. This is perhaps a controversial view after the great many requests there were to simplify the National Curriculum. It is true that the overall workload created by the imposition of the National Curriculum and the assessment arrangements needed addressing. However, it seems a shame that individual documents were not assessed for their quality. In part this is tied in with a view of the curriculum reflected by discrete subjects, where the cross-curricular links are no longer emphasized. By cross-curricular I mean the links that exist between the subjects of the National Curriculum, rather than issues such as citizenship.

The final section of this chapter looks in more detail at some of the specific quotes from the document that can be used to support the process approach, and particularly composition. This is not intended to imply that transcription is not addressed through the process approach. However, as I have argued, the process approach does have a particularly important contribution to make to the development of written composition.

Further specific links with the process approach to writing

General requirements for English: Key Stages 1–4

c To develop as effective writers, pupils should be taught to use:
  • compositional skills – developing ideas and communicating meaning to a reader, using a wide ranging vocabulary and an effective style, organizing and structuring sentences grammatically and whole texts coherently.

(Department for Education 1995: 2)

The use of the word 'skills' in 'compositional skills' is perhaps unfortunate. An understanding of composition is much more than the development of a set of skills. The development of composition significantly involves the development of concepts, for example awareness of audience preference; understanding of the social interactive nature of the publishing cycle; the ability to reflect on language structure; creative flair to generate interesting ideas; the confidence to redraft; etc. The important words in the general requirements are 'developing ideas'. I do not believe this is happening if the children are always given a stimulus. Nor do occasional sessions of free choice or 'creative writing' fulfil the need to improve the children's ability to develop ideas of high quality.

Key Stage 1 Programme of Study

Writing

• *1. Range*

  a Pupils should be helped to understand the value of writing as a means of remembering, communicating, organizing and developing ideas and information, and as a source of <u>enjoyment</u>. Pupils should be taught to write independently on subjects that are of interest and importance to them.

(Department for Education 1995: 9)

Key Stage 2 Programme of Study

Writing

- *1. Range*

  a Pupils should be given opportunities to write for varied purposes, understanding that writing is essential to thinking and learning, and enjoyable in itself.

  (Department for Education 1995: 15)

My own underlining indicates the importance of the idea that children should enjoy writing; achieving this is by no means a simple task. The process approach itself emerged as a result of feelings that children were not enjoying writing when it was presented as a relentless series of decontextualized activities from pupil workbooks, or through the over-use of stimuli such as story starters. If teachers are to develop enthusiasm in young writers they need to be enthusiastic themselves. Part of this enthusiasm comes from a commitment to developing progressive solutions to the problems of becoming a writer. It is simplistic to prescribe teaching and learning approaches without reference to children's motivation and interest in those approaches.

Key Stage 1

- *2. Key skills*

  b Pupils should have opportunities to plan and review their writing, assembling and developing their ideas on paper and on screen. Teachers should, on occasions, help pupils to compose at greater length by writing for them, demonstrating the ways that ideas may be recorded in print. To encourage confidence and independence, pupils should be given opportunities to collaborate, to read their work aloud and to discuss the quality of what is written.

  (Department for Education 1995: 9)

The reference to computers and perhaps overhead projectors is important. Teachers should make the distinction between packages that 'teach children how to write', and the use of a word processor as a tool. With the limited time for which children have access to computers in primary schools, it is preferable to develop an increasing sophistication with a word processor than to have the balance tilted towards writing skills development packages. A number of issues are referred to which are consistent with the practices of emergent writing and writing workshop: shared writing – 'help pupils to compose at greater length by writing for them . . . '; paired or collaborative writing – 'To encourage confidence and independence, pupils should be given opportunities to collaborate . . . '; sharing time – 'to read their work aloud and to discuss the quality of what is written'.

Key Stage 2

- *2. Key skills*

    b Pupils should be given the opportunities to plan, draft and improve their work on paper and on screen, and to discuss and evaluate their own and others' writing. To develop their writing, pupils should be taught to:

    - plan – note and develop initial ideas;
    - draft – develop ideas from the plan into structured written text;
    - revise – alter and improve the draft;
    - proof read – check the draft for spelling and punctuation errors, omissions or repetitions;
    - present – prepare a neat, correct and clear final copy.

    Pupils should be encouraged to develop their ability to organize and structure their writing in a variety of ways using their experience of fiction, poetry and other texts.

    (Department for Education 1995: 15)

This section of the National Curriculum for English is perhaps the clearest link with the use of writing workshop in the classroom. Although the various requirements can be taught individually, it is far easier to set up the process approach in the classroom using regular writing workshop sessions where the issues to do with planning, drafting and proofreading should be an ongoing feature of the work. It is interesting to note that although the document generally stresses the importance of a range of genres, the reference to fiction first is perhaps an indication that fiction does have a particularly important role in the development of writing.

Level descriptions

Attainment Target 3: Writing

- *Level 1*

    Pupils' writing communicates meaning through simple words and phrases.

- *Level 2*

    Pupils' writing communicates meaning in both narrative and non-narrative forms, using appropriate and interesting vocabulary, and showing some awareness of the reader.

- *Level 3*

    Pupils' writing is often organized, imaginative and clear. The main features of different forms of writing are used appropriately, beginning to be adapted to different readers. Sequences of sentences extend ideas logically and words are chosen for variety and interest.

- *Level 4*

  Pupils' writing in a range of forms is lively and thoughtful. Ideas are often sustained and developed in interesting ways and organized appropriately for the purpose and the reader. Vocabulary choices are often adventurous and words are used for effect. Pupils are beginning to use grammatically complex sentences, extending meaning.

  (Department for Education 1995: 20)

The level descriptions for compositional development are somewhat disappointing. Although I have shown that there are positive aspects to the requirements for English, the relative importance of the various sections is indicated by what is to be assessed. Motivation does not feature in the level descriptions, yet most teachers would be able to indicate what level of motivation individual children showed for writing. Indeed, this kind of observation often features in reports to parents. In part the disappointment is reflected in the difficulties of trying to map children's writing development onto a numbered scale. However, the limited language used to describe development is also a problem. Part of the answer to this lies in the greater use of teachers' observations and experience of children's writing development as the basis for such statements.

One of the benefits of the process approach is the opportunity it offers for critical reflection on the teaching and learning context. This kind of critical reflection needs to be part of teachers' response to the wider national picture as well. In this chapter I have shown that the use of the process approach can be clearly supported by the National Curriculum requirements. Although the National Curriculum was written primarily as a statement of curriculum content, in reality it is difficult to separate content from pedagogy. Because of the close links between content and pedagogy, teachers need to be confident to critically evaluate all statements of policy, not least those which are produced by national government.

TEN

The wider picture

This book has emphasized the practical possibilities of the process approach. In this chapter it is my intention to review some of the theory and research that relates to the practice. In common with a number of other writers, I consider that Donald Graves's work is the single most important influence on the development of the process approach. For this reason this chapter looks particularly at Graves's research and ideas, and some of his critics.

The process approach as a term and as a teaching approach has had a strong influence in Australia and the USA. In America this is reflected in the journal *Language Arts*. *Language Arts* is the journal for primary educators in the USA that is produced by the National Council for Teachers of English (NCTE): NCTE is equivalent to the National Association for Teachers of English (NATE) in the UK. In *Language Arts* the term 'process approach' is regularly used both as a focus for articles and as a well established concept that is frequently referred to.

As an example of such an article from *Language Arts* I refer to one by Sudol and Sudol (1991). They describe the experiences of Peg Sudol implementing the process approach in her classroom. The article describes how Peg Sudol (1991: 293) came to question her own skill-and-drill approach and 'committed herself to a writers' workshop'. She had two main worries during the year of evaluation. One of these was the problem she faced with a head who was sceptical of the approach; in the end she used test scores to show that the children's results were as good as the year before. The other worry related to her nagging doubt that she 'wasn't doing the workshop right'. This worry was alleviated by talking to a colleague in another school and comparing experiences. The article accepts three texts as 'the handbooks of the new pedagogy': *Writing: Teachers and Children at Work* (Graves 1983); *The Art of Teaching Writing* (Calkins 1986); and *In the Middle: Writing, Reading and Learning with Adolescents* (Atwell 1987). Of the three authors cited in the article, Donald Graves has had the strongest influence on the teaching of writing.

There is little doubt that Graves has been an influential figure in discussion on writing pedagogy. In addition to Sudol and Sudol, a range of writers allude to the influence of Graves's ideas. Czerniewska (1992: 85) described Graves as 'one of the most seductive writers in the history of writing pedagogy'. McKernan (1993), who worked with action research project leaders in the USA, Britain and Ireland, said that Graves was one of the authors most frequently referred to. Smagorinsky (1987: 340) suggested that 'the legion of teachers who employ it ['the Graves method'] would no doubt scoff at the suggestion that Graves's work is without merit'. In 'The Process of Writing' – a section of the Language in the National Curriculum (LINC) materials – Graves's book *Writing: Teachers and Children at Work* is described as 'the classic advocacy for a "process" approach to writing with an emphasis on the centrality of teacher-pupil conferencing' (LINC 1992: 148).

The National Writing Project and the LINC project

The National Writing Project in the UK had many examples of teachers using elements of the process approach. Pam Czerniewska used her experience as Director of the National Writing Project from 1985 to 1988 for her book *Learning About Writing* written in 1992. In a chapter on writing in the classroom she included some work done by a teacher in Avon.

The Avon class teacher Vera Pelley addressed the process approach by starting with a focus on 'audience'. She became dissatisfied with the time difficulties she encountered during this focus, and used drafting, editing and publishing as a way of giving her more time to respond to the children's work and interact with them. The notion of a specified audience for writing became a particularly strong influence on the teaching of writing in the UK, and it was emphasized by the National Writing Project. However, in the search for pre-planned and specified audiences there is a danger that the important contribution of the children in the class as a primary audience can be marginalized.

Czerniewska goes on to show how the work of Vera Pelley resulted in a particular sequence for the publication of the story books that were described.

1 Class discussion
2 First draft (the teacher also wrote one)
3 Revision (modelled first by looking at the teacher's draft)
4 Second draft (not necessarily a rewrite)
5 Consulting (in groups of three, children read and commented on drafts)
6 Third (usually final) draft
7 Editing (detailed correction, mainly of spelling and punctuation)
8 Preparation for publication (including layout and instructions for typist)
9 Illustrations
10 The cover

11   Binding
12   Reading the finished books to their audience

(Czerniewska 1992: 87)

This sequence serves as an example of how the UK has adopted the process approach in slightly different ways from some other countries. The teacher applied a definite structure to the production of the story books. The children were offered three titles, and a fourth choice where they could choose the subject. In the example, Pelley stated that having written an early draft of all four choices, 'almost all chose the story they had written for younger children' which was one of the teacher's suggestions. The writing activity was tightly structured by the process list above and through the list of titles. This level of detailed structure needs to be used sensitively, as it can detract from one of the most important aspects of the process approach, the child's autonomy.

The use of the process approach implies that children should choose the topic and form of their writing as long as they are making appropriate choices. Graves is quite clear on the issue.

> Children who are fed topics, story starters, lead sentences, even opening paragraphs as a steady diet for three or four years, rightfully panic when topics have to come from them . . . Writers who do not learn to choose topics wisely lose out on the strong link between voice and subject . . . The data show that writers who learn to choose topics well make the most significant growth in both information and skills at the point of best topic. With best topic the child exercises strongest control, establishes ownership, and with ownership, pride in the piece.
>
> (Graves 1983: 21)

I would qualify Graves's assertion by saying that if teachers wish to add further structure to the process approach they can do this in two ways. First, consider the balance between writing workshop and set writing tasks that happen at different times during the week. The structured process described by Pelley could have been done at a different time from the writing workshop. This would have kept the writing workshop as a special time, resulting in higher motivation from the children. Secondly, if children require a higher level of structure, this can be achieved without compromising the freedom of the workshop by giving the individual child the direction that they require. The statement, 'The data show that writers who learn to choose topics well make the most significant growth in both information and skills at the point of best topic' perhaps needs some further research. Graves seems to be implying that the writing skills such as spelling and handwriting develop more quickly when children choose a piece of writing that they are particularly interested in.

The LINC project also found the process approach to be an important contribution to discussions of writing pedagogy. The project involved most schools in England and Wales in an in-service project that focused on knowledge about the teaching and learning of language and literacy. The project took place between 1989 and 1992. Unfortunately, final publication of the materials was refused by politicians, as the materials perhaps did not fit comfortably with their view of the teaching of English. In spite of this, the materials were distributed, and various publications have resulted such as *Knowledge about Language and the Curriculum* by Ronald Carter (1990). One of the activities in the LINC materials describes the work of another Avon teacher. The focus of the activity was a piece of writing done by a child in the class called Kevin. As part of the introduction to the activity, information was given on the classroom context.

> Children in the class were actively encouraged to talk about their choice of subjects and their choice of audience as well as the form they were going to use . . . When the pieces of writing were completed they were put into a writing folder for possible display and later publication, perhaps in the form of booklets.
>
> (LINC 1992: 118)

This quote clearly indicates some of the issues that are addressed through use of the process approach. The children's autonomy is shown by their opportunity to choose subject, audience and form. Publication forms a natural possible conclusion to the writing process, with the writing folder used as a convenient organizational resource during the writing.

The National Writing Project and the LINC project were two of the most significant influences on UK writing pedagogy throughout the '80s and early '90s. Some of the ideas that were developed in these projects had a direct influence on the subsequent National Curriculum documentation. Unfortunately, the influence of the process approach on such documentation and classroom practice seems to exist as something of a compromise, so that although, for example, the notion of redrafting is part of the National Curriculum, pupil choice and autonomy is not so clearly required. It is this autonomy that can give purpose to redrafting and the process of writing itself.

Criticisms of Graves's work and the process approach

Smagorinsky (1987) is a rare critical voice in the context of Graves's work. His criticisms are particularly aimed at the research methods that Graves used in the 'New Hampshire Study'. Graves's (1981) New Hampshire study formed the research base for many of his ideas on the teaching of writing. Smagorinsky makes some searching observations on the methods that were used. His main criticism is that the biases of the researchers were allowed to influence the teachers and pupils that they observed. For example, Graves's enthusiasm for personal experience writing possibly resulted in his giving unconscious approval to this kind of writing. Smagorinsky also points out that Graves observed 30 children, but in 11 articles Graves refers to one child (Andrea) on 41 pages and only refers to one other student on more than ten pages.

In order to understand Smagorinsky's criticisms it is necessary to take a brief look at the two main research paradigms. Quantitative studies are generally 'scientific' in their approach. They set out a hypothesis and attempt to disprove or prove that it is sound. The use of statistics, mathematics and numbers is common in quantitative studies. Over the last 20 years the qualitative paradigm has established itself as an important alternative. Qualitative studies are characterized by in-depth observations of human activity. Case studies, field notes and researchers who participate at some level in the work of the people they are studying are common traits of qualitative studies. Qualitative researchers argue that it is possible to make generalizations from a single case study provided it is carried out in sufficient depth. The generalizations will be different from those possible with a large sample. In the field of writing, Glenda Bissex's (1980) study of her son Paul was one such single case study. The insights that her work gave teachers on the development of writing showed how influential single case studies can be.

It should be standard practice in qualitative studies – such as the one Graves carried out – for the biases of the researchers to be declared, and for reflection on these biases to form part of the reporting of the research. With qualitative research there is an inevitable problem when the researcher is both establishing and corroborating a finding. In relation to the declaration of bias, Smagorinsky perhaps makes a valid criticism of the New Hampshire study.

Smagorinsky does make some important points about Graves's methods, but overall he fails to demonstrate a proper understanding of qualitative methodology. For example, he suggests that Graves should have set up a 'control' to deal with the possibility of the researchers inadvertently giving approval to certain behaviours. He also suggests he lacks faith in the 'reliability' of Graves's findings. Both these concepts of 'control' and 'reliability' are predominantly applied in the context of quantitative studies.

The concept of control comes from quantitative research. Teachers probably remember the use of control in their secondary school science experiments. For example, if you were testing the effect of absence of light on a plant, you would include a control: that is, another plant that was put under the same conditions but had access to light. It is not possible to set up a control for qualitative studies because the researcher documents a unique moment in time. The actions of the people involved in the research setting are different on each occasion. Nor is it possible to set up an identical parallel group, because each person and group of people is unique.

The concept of 'reliability' also come from quantitative methods. Put simply, the experiment is repeated and, if the results are the same, it is deemed to be reliable. For the same reasons as those described in relation to controls, it is impossible to repeat qualitative studies. However, qualitative studies do include strenuous efforts to ensure that the findings are 'valid'. There is a wide range of techniques and strategies for ensuring that the findings are valid or 'trustworthy'. 'Pragmatic validity' (Miles and Huberman 1994) is one such technique. Pragmatic validity is an evaluation of the practical use of research findings; how accurate and useful do practitioners find the outcomes of a piece of research? On Smagorinsky's own admission there can be no doubt that Graves's research was successful by this criterion.

> The great number of elementary school teachers who implement their ideas and attend their [Graves's and his research workers'] conference presentations should easily attest to the effectiveness of many of their ideas.
>
> (Smagorinsky 1987: 333)

Smagorinsky is not the only critic of Graves's work and the process approach. During the '80s and up to current times, the 'genre theorists' have had a significant influence on writing pedagogy in the UK. The genre theorists too were critical of some of Graves's ideas. As the work of the genre theorists has had considerable influence, and because they offer criticisms of Graves, I include an analysis of their ideas.

Genre is usually regarded as a structural form. *Chambers English Dictionary* describes genre as 'a literary or artistic type or style'. For example, in music, genres include the symphony, the quartet and the concerto. In writing, genres include narrative, poetry, article, diary etc. However, the genre theorists have taken a much wider definition, which Martin *et al.* (1987: 59) expresses as a 'staged, goal oriented social process'. This wider definition allows the inclusion of genres that emphasize the spoken form as well as written forms, and includes consideration of the links between the two modes; so 'jokes, sermons, appointment making, anecdotes, weather reports' etc. are all included as examples of genres.

The three authors who perhaps have been referred to most in relation to genre theory are J. R. Martin, Frances Christie and Joan Rothery. One of the key texts from 1987 was *The Place of Genre in Learning*, where these three authors put forward some of their ideas as a response to other authors in the book. They also offered some criticisms of the process approach.

In a section of Martin *et al.*'s chapter they examine the notion of 'freedom' during the process approach. They ask a series of important questions:

> What is freedom? Is a progressive process writing classroom really free? Does allowing children to choose their own topics, biting one's tongue in conferences and encouraging ownership, actually encourage the development of children's writing abilities?
>
> (Martin *et al.* 1987: 77)

To answer these questions the authors report on a school in the Australian Northern Territory with a large population of Aboriginal children. They claimed that over the course of the year the children had only written about one of four topics: '(a) visiting friends and relatives; (b) going hunting for bush tucker; (c) sporting events; (d) movies or TV shows they have seen' (Martin *et al.* 1987: 77). This example is used to cast doubts on the effectiveness of the process approach. During the course of the present book I show that the process approach can have the opposite effect on the range of forms that Martin *et al.* refer to. (The chapter on writing workshop and Appendix 3 both offer a snapshot of the range of forms that children were involved in.) However, it is important that teachers monitor the range of writing and that they intervene positively to ensure that children are developing appropriately.

Martin *et al.*'s answer to the perceived problems of the process approach was didactic teaching on the structure and range of various genres that are available. For example, if the teacher were reading *Little Red Riding Hood* he/she might refer to the stages of a genre. In the narrative genre they suggest that these stages are 'Orientation, Complication and Resolution'. Later in the chapter they suggest that these could be added to: 'Abstract/Orientation/ Complication/Evaluation/Resolution/Coda'. To further complicate matters, they add additional story genres.

> Martin and Rothery (1981) distinguish as well recount, which lacks a Complication (and thus a Resolution), and thematic narrative, in which recurring Complication Resolution sequences might be used to articulate a literary theme. Subsequently Martin (1984b) reviewed in addition: the moral tale, myth, spoof, and serial. This seven-genre framework has to date proved adequate for characterizing story writing in Australian infant and primary schools.
>
> (Martin *et al*. 1987: 74)

The authors do make an important point about the necessity for teachers to refer to the larger text structures. This means talking directly to children about the building blocks of the various written forms. But their suggestions are severely limited by the lack of direct examples of how teachers and children might respond to the complex demands represented by the kind of language they use to describe, for example, the structure of *Little Red Riding Hood*. The authors are not suggesting that teachers use their terminology, but there is little discussion of how teachers might adapt the complex language and ideas, how children might respond, and the nature of the benefits, for children's writing development. The authors' difficulty in empathizing with the work of teachers and children runs throughout the writing and calls into question their in-depth experience of the teaching and learning of primary children.

The last point is illustrated by a specific criticism the genre theorists make of Graves's work. They examine an extract from *Writing: Teachers and Children at Work*.

Mr Sitka: What is this paper about, Anton?

Anton: Well, I'm not sure. At first I thought it was going to be about when we won the game in overtime with the penalty kick. But when I got going on how our team had won because we were in such good shape for overtime. You see, the other team hardly move at the end. Took me way back to our earlier practices when I hated the coach so much. Gosh, I don't know what it's about.

Mr Sitka: Where are you now in the draft?

Anton: Oh, I've just got the part down about when we won in overtime.

Mr Sitka: So, you've just got started then. Well, it's probably too early to tell what it's about. What did you figure to do with the next draft then?

Anton: I don't know. I don't want to just write and wander around. I've written about when we've won but it just sort of has me stuck at that point.

Mr Sitka: Tell me about that coach of yours.

Anton: God, how I hated him! I almost quit three or four times maybe. I thought he couldn't stand me. He'd yell, catch every little thing I did wrong. We'd run and run until we couldn't stand up. Have some passing drills. Then he'd run us some more. He'd just stand

there yellin' and puffin' on his cigar. Course he was right. When
we won the championship, I think it went right back to those
early practices.

Mr Sitka: The way you tell it sounds as though you have quite a live
beginning to your story. Try writing about early practices, then
see what your piece is about.

(Graves 1983: 114)

Martin *et al.* cite this extract as an example of 'unfocussed conferencing'. They
criticize the teacher for not directly helping the young writer to 'shape the
structure of his narrative'. They go on to suggest that this kind of indirect guidance will only benefit bright middle class children who are 'sure to read
between the lines and learn to write, apparently effortlessly, without being
taught'.

Their criticisms reflect a distorted view of effective teaching and learning. In
the extract the pupil does the bulk of the talking. It seems that the teacher has
developed a good working relationship, as the pupil is confident enough to
express a range of ideas and issues. The teacher is clearly encouraging the pupil
to think independently, and resists telling him what to do. Instead he encourages the pupil to reflect on, and begin to solve, some of his own problems. The
charge that the teacher does nothing to directly help the writer shape the
narrative is plainly mistaken. Each of the teacher's questions directs the writer's
attention to important aspects of the written structure, such as the theme of
the writing; the direction of the piece; where the pupil is in the process; a
potentially interesting addition to the plot; how the piece might begin. The
teacher's final piece of dialogue does just what Martin *et al.* say the teacher
does not do; i.e. directly help the writer with the structure: 'The way you tell
it sounds as though you have quite a live beginning to your story. Try writing
about early practices, then see what your piece is about.' The teacher offers
some focused positive feedback designed to support the pupil's self-esteem and
to signal a potentially effective opening to the narrative. The teacher is quite
clear in the suggestion that Anton should use the 'early practices' as the beginning of the story. Following this suggestion the teacher presumably feels that
Anton is capable of taking that opening further, so he does not offer other
specific recommendations. However, the teacher would of course be aware that
later on he might return if Anton struggles with the next section, but he has
at least given him the opportunity to solve the next problem himself.

The genre theorists themselves have been the subject of other considerable
criticism. Myra Barrs (1991) puts forward an acid deconstruction of genre
theory that highlights some of the naiveté and authoritarianism of the genre
theorists. Barrs acknowledges that the focus on the larger textual structures
that Kress (1982: 97) calls 'larger structures within which sentences occur' is
welcome, but she is scathing in her criticism of the genre theorists. She suggests that they take a particularly negative view of children's emerging compositions and justify this by reference to adult notions of genre. They fail to
show a credible understanding of children's writing development. This negative view is accompanied by a tone that is hardly likely to endear the genre
theorists to the people they are trying to persuade, namely teachers.

Rothery and her colleagues all too readily take up the roles of telling, asserting, pronouncing and positively laying down the law . . . It is hard to see how children are to be either informed or empowered by teaching approaches which are insensitive to children's attempts, and as relentlessly didactic as those implied in many of the writings of the genre school.

(Barrs 1991: 12)

One of Barrs's final criticisms is perhaps the most damning; it is that the genre theorists fail to take a suitably rigorous and self critical view of their own theories; for example, there are few attempts to describe things tentatively or to search for opposing evidence of their claims. This reveals itself in their lack of references to other researchers who are working in related fields, and their reliance on authors working within the genre theory field itself.

Cairney (1992) also has some concerns about the genre debate. Like Barrs, he suggests that the definition of what genre is and how different genres are structured is problematic. He questions how uniform the various genres remain over time. Just as the vocabulary of the language is constantly changing, is this not the case with genre? One only needs to look at the Internet for an example of a huge range of new or modified genres. Consider the differences in tone and style between an e-mail message and a posted letter. Cairney (1992: 29) suggests that 'to define them too dogmatically is to run the risk of imposing on writers sanitized forms. The history of writing suggests that genres change, and at times are deliberately modified for writer effect.'

Cairney also refers to the didacticism implicit in much of the writing of the genre theorists. He cites Graves's work as a positive example of children who write with greater power when given 'control' of their writing. The notion of control is extremely important in the context of the process approach. It spans all the issues from the child to the school and the wider community. The process approach, when used effectively, offers children a balance of control that enables them to learn to write ultimately with greater motivation and in greater depth.

There have also been some problems with the process approach at a practical level. Some teachers have taken Graves's ideas and applied them in a mechanistic way. The flexibility and individualized nature of the approach has been replaced by an insistence, for example, that children always carry out a set series of drafts. This misunderstanding of drafting has also been evident in situations where teachers and children have seen drafting as a 'rough copy–neat copy' process. The drafting involved is at such a low level that it quickly becomes a boring routine. The LINC materials recognized this problem in the chapter on 'The Process of Writing'.

There has been a tendency, strongly resisted in some quarters, to elevate Graves's ideas into a system for teaching writing. This has led, in some interpretations of his ideas, to an inflexibility whereby pupils are required to write a given number of drafts, instead of providing the flexibility that should liberate pupils from the constraints of one draft writing.

(LINC 1992: 150)

There can also be a problem with 'writing workshop' if it is used too often in relation to other set writing tasks. Calkins (1986: 25) recommends that 'teachers set aside an hour a day, every day, for the writing workshop'. There are problems with this recommendation in relation to the other areas of the curriculum that need to be fitted in. I feel that writing workshop works best when other writing tasks enhance the development of skills and concepts that in turn are used in the writing workshop. The important feature of this relationship is that the process writing is used to inspire the development of other relevant set writing activities linked to the needs of the children. This means that writing workshop can be timetabled as little as once a week, but the philosophies that underpin the process approach inform many other activities that take place.

Finally, some advocates of the process approach have perhaps exaggerated the teacher's role as a facilitator. If a correct balance is not found between encouraging children to think for themselves and direct teacher intervention, some children can struggle to learn effectively. There will always be a minority of children who require different levels of intervention. One positive aspect of the process approach is that it gives the teacher the opportunity to see any problems that the children may have and deal with them in an individualized way.

I have given an overview of some of the important theories and research that have contributed to understanding of the process approach. The process approach has had widespread appeal and has been shown to have positive effects on the development of children's writing. In spite of the objective and anecdotal evidence that the process approach offers great potential in the teaching of writing, it is still an approach that is only used by small numbers of schools and teachers. Like any approach, it cannot answer all the questions that teachers have about the learning of writing; but when genuinely balanced with other approaches, it can be an exciting method for motivating children and teachers, and for improving children's writing.

Modifications to PLR writing sample

WRITING OBSERVATIONS			
Child's name:		**Year group:**	
	Observation one *Date:*	*Observation two* *Date:*	*Observation three* *Date:*
Context: • Title and genre • Pupil choice or teacher task • Alone or in collaboration • Level of support	Poem – musical/sound/colour. Teacher task. Kevin worked individually on this. I was available for all pupils to assist – with ideas and spellings using word books.		
Composition: • Generating ideas • Understanding of genre • Use of language • Awareness of reader • Influences used • Drafting skills	Kevin demonstrated that he has a creative imagination. He understood what I had asked him to do. Showed he possesses a wide knowledge of vocabulary. I initiated the activity and gave the children a demonstration of what I wanted.		
Transcription: • Spelling • Punctuation • Handwriting	40/50 spellings standard. No evidence of punctuation. Neatly printed writing which showed he had good letter formation.		

	Observation one Date:	Observation two Date:	Observation three Date:
Child's own view of their writing:	Pleased with it – proud – type it on 'Pendown' [computer] for display.		
Future action:	Kevin is ready to use simple punctuation – capital letters and full stops.		

Language policy contents list

School 1

Writing
Statements of our philosophy
What is writing? When does it begin?
Four examples of early writing
'Language stories and literacy lessons'
Physical organization of the classroom
Pencil control
A selection of strategies
'Helping children make progress in spelling'
'Survive day one'
'Talking about writing'
'What we need when we write'
Child choice
Composition
'Who is the writer doing it for?'
Spelling strategies
Reminders for spelling
'Catchwords'
Spelling development
Writing concepts
Spelling issues
The history of spelling

Reading
Classroom organization
Reading record
An environment for supporting language learning
Using stories to support emergent writers
The four cueing systems
Encouraging reading for meaning
Texts
Miscue analysis

'Racism and reading schemes'
Phonics
Reading scale data and analysis
Reading scales

Talking
This section was under development

School 2

Writing
The beginnings of writing
More experienced writers
Transcription
   Spelling
   Handwriting

Reading
The choice of texts
Reading diaries
Interacting with children

Appendices
Spelling strategies
Spelling games
Core book list with short reviews
Sample reading diary observations
Quotes from national policy documents supporting approach

School 3

Aims
Objectives
What is language?
Equal opportunities
Special educational needs

Speaking
Aims
Objectives

Listening
Aims
Objectives
The role of the teacher
Assessment
Resources

Reading
Aims
Objectives
The role of the teacher
The school library
Parental involvement

Assessment
Resources

Writing
Aims
Objectives
The role of the teacher

Spelling
Aim
Objectives
The role of the teacher

Handwriting
Aim
Objectives
The role of the teacher
Assessment
Resources
Liaison

Bibliography

Appendices
Reading records

APPENDIX III

Snapshot of writing workshop pieces

Poems, stories and jokes.

Sarah and the vegetarian fox. Based on the book *Whoever Heard of a Vegetarian Fox?* Using the character of the fox but with other new characters.

Water safety poster; idea from topic on water. Card for mother.

Collaborative project that had to be kept secret until finished.

Information book about hamsters. Child had hamster at home and wanted to give other people some information.

Finishing very long first book of the year. Story called 'Escape from the Desert'. Wants to write an information book on gerbils next.

'Deceos and the Three Eyed Giant'. Collaborative writing of a Greek myth. Idea came from topic and class reading of myths and legends.

Book of games. Wanted a book that would involve much drawing, as the child was good at this. Making up a series of traditional type games.

'Tommy's Adventure'. Idea came from 'Jumanji'. 'Robin Williams goes through a forest and he meets lots of animals and dangers; funny film.'

'Mr Magnificent'. Wanted an 'exciting' story. Short name is 'Mr M'; at the end becomes 'Sir Magnificent'.

Information about Islam. Idea from teacher. Child was stuck for a new idea, having completed a joke book at home on the computer.

A book of mazes; collaborative project. Initially a temporary plan because another piece of writing had been left at home.

Worked on a complex maze at home inspired by the work on ancient Greece. Now writing a book of mazes with instructions.

Completing the final draft of a book of three short stories. Started at the beginning of the year and continued both at home and school.

Andy the Pandy comic. First story is 'Hiss the Snake', second is 'Leo the Lion'.

'Fish and Chip'. Football comedy that has been worked on since beginning of year.

'The Funny Ones'. Sam, Bob, Chris and Nick find an island in the Pacific Ocean.

'The Grass Gods'. Long and complex story based on adventure game format. Each chapter represents a different level.

'Laugh Times One'. Joke book. Idea from joke book given by brother.

Just finished 'The Missing Page', currently brainstorming for new idea.

Information book about dinosaurs. Follows information book about the human body.

Collaborative project: 'The Nerds'. Characters taken from sweet packets.

'Little Dracula'. Based on cartoon.

Information book about a range of different pets.

References

Adams, M.J. (1990) *Beginning to Read: The New Phonics in Context. A Précis of the Classic Text.* Oxford: Heinemann.

Ahlberg, J. and Ahlberg, A. (1986) *The Jolly Postman or Other People's Letters.* London: Heinemann.

Atwell, N. (1987) *In the Middle: Writing, Reading and Learning with Adolescents.* Portsmouth, New Hampshire: Heinemann Educational Books.

Barrs, M. (1990) Children's themes of narrative. *English in Education,* 24(1): 32–9.

Barrs, M. (1991) Genre theory: what's it all about? *Language Matters,* 1991/92(1): 9–16.

Barrs, M. and Pidgeon, S. (eds) (1993) *Reading the Difference.* London: Centre for Language in Primary Education.

Barrs, M., Ellis, S., Hester, H. and Thomas, A. (1989) *The Primary Language Record Handbook.* London: ILEA/CLPE.

Beard, R. (1984) *Children's Writing in the Primary School.* Sevenoaks: Hodder and Stoughton.

Bereiter, C. and Scardamalia, M. (1982) From conversation to composition, in R. Glaser (ed.) *Advances in Instructional Psychology, Volume 2.* New Jersey: Lawrence Erlbaum Associates.

Bereiter, C. and Scardamalia, M. (1987) *The Psychology of Written Composition.* Hillsdale, New Jersey: Lawrence Erlbaum Associates. Quoted in R. Beard (ed.), *Teaching Literacy Balancing Perspectives* (London: Hodder and Stoughton, 1993) 159, 162.

Bissex, G.L. (1980) *GNYS AT WRK: A Child Learns to Write and Read.* Cambridge, Massachusetts: Harvard University Press.

Bridge, M. (1990) Learning to read – a two year study of beginner readers, in B. Wade (ed.) *Reading for Real.* Buckingham: Open University Press.

Britton, J. (1970) *Language and Learning.* Harmondsworth: Penguin Books Ltd.

Browne, A. (1993) *Helping Children to Write.* London: Paul Chapman.

Browne, A. (1996) *Developing Language and Literacy 3–8.* London: Paul Chapman.

Burman, C. (1990) Support for real reading, in B. Wade (ed.) *Reading for Real.* Buckingham: Open University Press.

Cairney, T. (1992) Mountain or mole hill: the genre debate viewed from 'Down Under'. *Reading,* 26(1): 23–9.

Caldwell, B.J. and Spinks, M. (1988) *The Self Managing School*. Hove: Falmer Press. Quoted in P. Hann, The Role of the Language Coordinator. *Language Matters*, 1995/1996(1): 5–10.

Calkins, L.M. (1986) *The Art of Teaching Writing*. Portsmouth, New Hampshire: Heinemann Educational Books.

Campbell, R. (1992) *Reading Real Books*. Buckingham: Open University Press.

Carter, R. (1990) *Knowledge about Language and the Curriculum*. London: Hodder and Stoughton.

Cato, V., Fernandes, C., Gorman, T., Kispal, A. with White, J. (1992) *The Teaching of Initial Literacy: How do Teachers do it?* Slough: NFER.

Centre for Language in Primary Education (1996) The New Primary Language Record Writing Scale. *Language Matters*, 1995/1996(3): 3–8.

Clay, M.M. (1989) *The Early Detection of Reading Difficulties (third edition)*. Auckland: Heinemann.

Cripps, C. and Peters, M.L. (1990) *Catchwords Ideas for Teaching Spelling*. London: Harcourt Brace Jovanovich.

Cusick, R.T. (1991) *April Fools*. London: Scholastic.

Czerniewska, P. (1992) *Learning about Writing*. Oxford: Blackwell.

Department for Education (1995) *Key Stages 1 and 2 of the National Curriculum*. London: HMSO.

Dougill, P. (1993) *The Primary Language Book*. Buckingham: Open University Press.

Ferreiro, E. and Teberosky, A. (1982) *Literacy before Schooling*. Portsmouth, New Hampshire: Heinemann Educational Books.

Gentry, J.R. (1981) Learning to spell developmentally. *Reading Teacher*, 34(4): 378–81.

Gorman, T., White, J., Brooks, G. and English, F. (1989) *Language for Learning, a Summary Report on the 1988 APU Surveys of Language Performance*. London: HMSO.

Graves, D.H. (1981) Patterns of child control of the writing process, in D. Graves (ed.) *A Case Study Observing the Development of Primary Children's Composing, Spelling, and Motor Behaviours during the Writing Process, Final Report*. Durham: University of New Hampshire.

Graves, D.H. (1983) *Writing: Teachers and Children at Work*. Portsmouth, New Hampshire: Heinemann Educational Books.

Gray, B. (1983) A survey of books used in Northern Ireland to teach beginners to read. *The Northern Teacher*, 14(1): 28–32.

Gundlach, R.A. (1981) On the nature and development of children's writing, in C.H. Frederiksen and J.F. Dominic (eds) *Writing: the Nature, Development, and Teaching of Written Communication (Volume 2)*. New Jersey: Lawrence Erlbaum Associates.

Hall, N. (1987) *The Emergence of Literacy*. Sevenoaks: Hodder and Stoughton.

Hall, N. and Robinson, A. (eds) (1996) *Learning about Punctuation*. Clevedon: Multilingual Matters.

Hann, P. (1996) The role of the language coordinator. *Language Matters*, 1995/1996 (1): 5–10.

Harrison, C. (1992) The reading process and learning to read: what a teacher using a 'real books' approach needs to know, in C. Harrison and M. Coles (eds) *The Reading for Real Handbook*. London: Routledge.

Harrison, C. and Coles, M. (1992) *The Reading for Real Handbook*. London: Routledge.

Harste, J.C., Woodward, V.A. and Burke, C.L. (1984) *Language Stories and Literacy Lessons*. Portsmouth, New Hampshire: Heinemann Educational Books.

Haviland, J. (1988) *Take Care, Mr Baker!* London: Fourth Estate.

Hepburn, J. (1991) Spelling categories and strategies. *Reading*, 25(1): 33–7.

Holdaway, D. (1979) *The Foundations of Literacy*. London: Ashton Scholastic.

Hughes, T. (1968) *The Iron Man*. London: Faber and Faber.

Jarman, C. (1979) *The Development of Handwriting Skills*. London: Simon and Schuster.

Johnson, P. (1990) *A Book of One's Own: Developing Literacy Through Making Books*. London: Hodder and Stoughton.

Kress, G. (1982) *Learning to Write*. London: Routledge and Kegan Paul.

Language in the National Curriculum (LINC) (1992). *Materials for Professional Development* (Unpublished).

Laycock, E. (1990) Fifteen months in the life of a writer (teacher inquiry in the classroom). *Language Arts*, 67(2): 206–17.

Martin, J.R., Christie, F. and Rothery, J. (1987) Social processes in education: a reply to Sawyer and Watson (and others), in I. Reid (ed.) *The Place of Genre in Learning*. Victoria: Deakin University.

McKernan, J. (1993) Varieties of curriculum action research: constraints and typologies in American, British and Irish projects. *Journal of Curriculum Studies*, 25(5): 445–57.

Meek, M. (1988) *How Texts Teach What Readers Learn*. Stroud: Thimble Press.

Miles, M.B. and Huberman, A.M. (1994) *Qualitative Data Analysis: An Expanded Sourcebook*. London: Sage.

Mudd, N. (1994) *Effective Spelling: A Practical Guide for Teachers*. London: Hodder and Stoughton.

The National Writing Project (1989) *Becoming a Writer*. Walton-on-Thames: Nelson.

Parker, S. (1993) *The Craft of Writing*. London: Paul Chapman.

Payton, S. (1984) *Developing Awareness of Print: A Young Child's First Steps Towards Literacy*. University of Birmingham: Educational Review.

Peters, M. (1985) *Spelling Caught or Taught: A New Look (revised edition)*. London: Routledge.

Peters, M. (1991) Spelling and the National Curriculum. *Links*, 16(3): 36–40.

Reid, I. (ed.) (1987) *The Place of Genre in Learning*. Victoria: Deakin University.

Reid, J. (1993) Reading and spoken language: the nature of the links, in R. Beard (ed.) *Teaching Literacy Balancing Perspectives*. London: Hodder and Stoughton.

Rice, I. (1987) Racism and reading schemes, the current situation. *Reading*, 21(2): 92–7.

Sassoon, R. (1990) *Handwriting – the Way to Teach It*. Cheltenham: Stanley Thornes.

Sciezka, J. (1989) *The True Story of the 3 Little Pigs! By A. Wolf*. London: Puffin Books.

Smagorinsky, P. (1987) Graves revisited: a look at the methods and conclusions of the New Hampshire study. *Written Communication*, 4(4): 331–42.

Smith, F. (1978) *Reading (second edition)*. Cambridge: Cambridge University Press.

Smith, F. (1982) *Writing and the Writer*. Portsmouth, New Hampshire: Heinemann Educational Books.

Stierer, B. (1995) Making a statement: an analysis of teacher/pupil talk within 'child conferences' in the Primary Language Record. *The Curriculum Journal*, 6(3): 343–62.

Sudol, D. and Sudol, P. (1991) Another story: putting Graves, Calkins, and Atwell into practice and perspective. *Language Arts*, 68(4): 292–300.

Sutcliffe, C. (1991) Can we have the writing games? An investigation into possible teacher intervention strategies in the development of young writers. *English in Education*, 25(2): 52–61.

Temple, C., Nathan, R., Burris, N. and Temple, F. (1982) *The Beginnings of Writing (second edition)*. Newton, Massachusetts: Allyn and Bacon.

Tizard, B. (1993) Early influences on literacy, in R. Beard (ed.) *Teaching Literacy Balancing Perspectives*. London: Hodder and Stoughton.

Tizard, B. and Hughes, M. (1984) *Young Children Learning*. London: Fontana.

Wade, B. (1990) *Reading for Real*. Milton Keynes: Open University Press.

Waterland, L. (1985) *Read With Me: An Apprenticeship Approach to Reading*. Stroud: Thimble Press.

Wells, G. (1986) *The Meaning Makers: Children Learning Language and Using Language to Learn*. Sevenoaks: Hodder and Stoughton.

White, J. (1989) Children's writing: some findings from data collected longitudinally. *Research Papers in Education*, 4(2): 53–78.

Wray, D. (1994) Reviewing the reading debate, in D. Wray and J. Medwell (eds) *Teaching Primary English: The State of the Art*. London: Routledge.

Index

STARTING FROM THE CHILD?
TEACHING AND LEARNING FROM 4 TO 8

Julie Fisher

Early years practitioners currently face a number of dilemmas when planning an education for young children. The imposition of an external curriculum seems to work in opposition to the principles of planning experiences which start from the child. Does this mean that the notion of a curriculum centred on the needs and interests of children is now more rhetoric than reality?

In a practical and realistic way *Starting from the Child?* examines a range of theories about young children as learners and the implications of these theories for classroom practice. Julie Fisher acknowledges the competence of young children when they arrive at school, the importance of building on their early successes and the critical role of adults who understand the individual and idiosyncratic ways of young learners. The book addresses the key issues of planning and assessment, explores the place of talk and play in the classroom and examines the role of the teacher in keeping a balance between the demands of the curriculum and the learning needs of the child.

This is essential reading, not only for early years practitioners, but for all those who manage and make decisions about early learning.

Contents
Competent young learners – Conversations and observations – Planning for learning – The role of the teacher – Encouraging independence – Collaboration and cooperation – The place of play – The negotiated classroom – Planning, doing and reviewing – Evaluation and assessment – References – Index.

192pp   0 335 19556 3 (Paperback)   0 335 19557 1 (Hardback)

READ IT TO ME NOW! (SECOND EDITION)
LEARNING AT HOME AND AT SCHOOL

Hilary Minns

- What do young children from different cultural backgrounds learn about reading and writing before they come to school?
- How can schools work with parents to incorporate children's pre-school literacy learning into policies for the development of literacy?
- What strategies can early years' teachers use to support young children's understanding of the reading process?

Read it to me now! charts the emergent literacy learning of five 4-year-old children from different cultural backgrounds in their crucial move from home to school, and demonstrates how children's early understanding of reading and writing is learnt socially and culturally within their family and community. Drawing the children's stories together, Hilary Minns discusses the role of the school in recognizing and developing children's literacy learning, including that of emergent bilingual learners, and in developing genuine home–school links with families. This edition of *Read it to me now!* makes reference to current texts that take knowledge and ideas of children's literacy learning further, and includes discussion of the literacy requirements of the National Curriculum.

Contents
Introduction – Part 1: Five children – Gurdeep – Gemma – Anthony – Geeta – Reid – Part 2: Further considerations – Learning to read – The role of story in young children's lives – Reading partnerships – Pathways to reading – References and further reading – Index.

176pp   0 335 19761 2 (Paperback)   0 335 19762 0 (Hardback)